# Praise for Charles Platt's *The Whole-Truth Home Computer Handbook:*

"I cannot recommend this book too highly. It is the only computer book I have read in a single sitting." *(Computer Weekly)*

"Loaded with information as well as warnings. Almost always, Platt is easily understandable...his book is a good one." *(Chicago Sun-Times)*

"Much sensible information presented in user-friendly mode." *(Washington Post)*

"One of the best introductions to the principles and practice of computing that I have come across." *(The Bookseller*, England)

"Platt uses his excellent sense of humor to help demystify computers and reduce the intimidation neophytes invariably experience." *(New York Post)*

*Other Avon Books by*
**Charles Platt**

THE WHOLE-TRUTH HOME COMPUTER HANDBOOK

# More from your Micro

CHARLES PLATT

AVON
PUBLISHERS OF BARD, CAMELOT, DISCUS AND FLARE BOOKS

MORE FROM YOUR MICRO is an original publication of Avon Books. This work has never before appeared in book form.

AVON BOOKS
A division of
The Hearst Corporation
1790 Broadway
New York, New York 10019


Published by arrangement with the author
Library of Congress Catalog Card Number: 84-91236
ISBN: 0-380-89529-3



First Avon Printing, March, 1985



Printed in the U.S.A.

WFH 10 9 8 7 6 5 4 3 2 1

# CONTENTS

# INTRODUCTION

Like many people, I bought a personal computer without knowing exactly what I was going to do with it. I was so intoxicated with the idea of owning an "electronic brain" that I didn't wonder too much about the practical applications.

My intoxication wore off, and turned into a high-tech hangover, when I went shopping for software to run on my new toy. I discovered:

- Most word-processing programs were awkward and inconvenient to use, and none of them offered the exact features that I wanted.
- Most video games turned out to be monotonous variations on the same old theme of little blobs chasing each other and blowing each other up.
- Programs to handle household tasks such as income taxes or name-and-address lists were less efficient than a pocket calculator or a box of file cards.
- A lot of commercially sold programs were badly designed or even defective. They didn't do what I wanted them to do. And they were too expensive.

Baffled and disillusioned, I turned to computer magazines, and books like this one, offering program listings that I could type myself. But this experience was even more disappointing. The programs turned out to be crude games that moved slowly and looked ugly—or they were arithmetical exercises of no use to anyone. For instance, I really didn't see the point of typing and running a program to convert Fahrenheit temperatures to Celsius.

My eventual answer was to become a part-time programmer myself. Before too long, I was designing and producing programs that *would* do what I wanted.

I ended up with a wide variety, including my own word-processing program and an elaborate data-base system. Some of these programs are too long and complex for this book and have been published and distributed commercially on disks. Others, however, are short and simple, yet no less useful; they are the ones that I have collected here.

These programs were not written as exercises, nor were they fabricated just to fill a few pages. They were devised either to be truly useful or truly entertaining. Unlike other books of programs, this one has been compiled selectively and is designed to be of lasting interest.

## Will They Work on Your Computer?

Books like this one usually claim the programs will work on "most popular computers," with maybe a tiny alteration here and there. Often this claim simply isn't true. The BASIC computer language has never been properly standardized, and different manufacturers use radically different versions of it. Converting a program to run on your particular system can be difficult, or even impossible. For instance, a program that uses DATA statements is never going to run on a Timex/Sinclair 1000 because that computer uses a version of BASIC in which the word DATA does not exist.

When I planned this book, I was determined not to cheat readers in this way. The programs here really will run on the most popular home computers, and where any alteration is necessary, I explain *precisely* what needs to be done.

Unfortunately, the versions of BASIC that Atari, Texas Instruments, and Timex/Sinclair use are so idiosyncratic that conversion is impractical. If you own one of these brands, I'm sorry to say that this book is not for you.

I designed my programs so that they will run on all these other brands:

Adam
Apple II, II-plus, IIe, and IIc
Columbia
Commodore 64 and VIC-2Ø
Compaq
Eagle
Franklin Ace
IBM PC and Pc*jr*
Kaypro
Osborne
TRS-8Ø
Zenith

Any other computer that uses Microsoft BASIC should also be compatible.

Although these computers use similar versions of BASIC, they do not display graphics in a standard format. This is no problem for programs that only display text, but five of the programs in this book do require graphics, so I have devised a "conversion routine" that customizes them automatically for your particular computer. You'll find instructions relating to this routine in Chapter 12, at the beginning of Part 5, *Games and Graphics.* You *must* read these instructions before trying to type any of the programs in that section of the book. Otherwise, those programs won't work.

## No Experience Necessary

For the novice computer user, Chapter 1 explains how to get your computer ready for writing programs, and Chapter 2 lists the few BASIC words in this book that vary from one computer to another. That's really all you need to know to start typing your first listing; you don't have to understand how a program actually works.

On the other hand, if you don't know anything about BASIC, you'll have trouble tracking down typing errors that stop your program from running properly, and you won't be able to modify your programs to suit your particular needs. For these reasons, if you have time, I suggest you read a simple, general instruction to BASIC in conjunction with this book. I've written such a guide myself, titled *BASIC Without Math,* but any general guide will do.

## Getting Started

At this point, you should:

- Plug in and switch on your computer, video monitor or television, and cassette recorder or disk drive.
- Get BASIC running on your computer; read Chapter 1 if you don't already know how.
- Be ready to save and load programs. Check your computer manual if you're not sure about this.

• Have a cassette tape or formatted blank disk ready, so you can save the programs that you write.

• Check on any small variations between modern Microsoft BASIC and BASIC on your computer, as listed in Chapter 2.

Then get to work. Copy-typing a program isn't much fun, but it has three tremendous advantages compared with buying software off the shelf.

1. You save a lot of money. For the price of this book, you get 15 programs that would cost $5 to $3Ø *each* if you bought them on disk or tape.
2. If you read the commentary that precedes each listing, you'll learn how the programs function.
3. You can use your new knowledge to adapt each program to your own tastes and needs. This is often impossible with commercial software, which is either copy-protected or written in a language other than BASIC.

The programs in this book helped to cure my high-tech hangover and enabled me to get much more use and fun out of my microcomputer. I hope the same will be true for you.

*P.S.* For those of you who are slow typists and find the long listings too much to handle, a shortcut is now available. I am offering *all* the programs in this book prerecorded on one disk, for IBM PC and PC*jr*, Apple II, or Commodore 64. You will still be able to list the programs, see how they work, and modify them, using the instructions in this book. You are simply saved the labor of typing.

For your disk, send $15 to Charles Platt, P.O. Box 556, New York, NY 1Ø113. Do *not* write to Avon Books.

# PART 1
# PRELIMINARIES

# CHAPTER 1
# BASIC FACTS FOR BEGINNERS

This chapter explains what a program is and how to begin typing BASIC on some popular home computers. If you already know how to do this, skip to Chapter 2.

## Starting Your System

Some computers allow you to type BASIC commands as soon as the machine has been switched on. Others require you to load the BASIC language from a disk. Here's the start-up procedure for the most popular models made by IBM, Apple, Commodore, and Radio Shack. If you own some other kind of computer, check your instruction manual. Remember, this book is not designed for use with Atari, Texas Instruments, or Timex/Sinclair computers.

***IBM PC:*** If you use your IBM PC with a cassette recorder, simply turn the computer on. Disk users must insert the system disk (also called the DOS disk) in the left-hand disk drive (if you have two drives); *then* turn on the computer; enter the time and date when the computer tells you to; when you see an A > symbol on the screen, type **BASICA** and press the Enter key to tell the computer to load Advanced BASIC from its disk.

You can now remove that disk and substitute the blank disk on which you will be saving your programs. Read your manual if you don't know how to *format* that disk before you begin work.

***Apple II:*** On newer models with the autostart routine, insert your system disk (also called the DOS disk) in the disk drive, if you have one, before you turn on the computer. On older models, do a system reset by pressing the Break key, then type **Control-B** to activate BASIC, and press the Return key. When you see some text on the screen followed by a square bracket, the system is ready. If you see a > instead of a square bracket, you are running Integer BASIC instead of Applesoft BASIC. Integer BASIC is not sufficient for the programs in this book. Check your manual for further details. Disk users must create a blank, formatted disk on which to save programs.

***Commodore 64 and VIC-2Ø:*** These computers are ready to run BASIC as soon as they are switched on. If you will be saving your programs on a disk, be sure it has been formatted before you begin work. See your disk-drive manual for details about the **NEWØ:** command.

***TRS-8Ø models II, III, and 4:*** If the computer asks **MEMORY SIZE?** when you turn it on, simply press the Return key. You're now ready to write programs in BASIC. If you will be saving your programs on a disk, read your your manual to find out how to *format* the disk before you start work.

## Ready Prompt

The Ready prompt is the word or symbol that appears on the screen when the computer is ready for you to type BASIC instructions. You cannot begin until you see this prompt. Here's how it looks on different computers:

*IBM:* **Ok**
*Apple:* **]**
*Commodore:* **READY**
*TRS-80:* **READY** with **>** sign underneath

Immediately following the Ready prompt you will see a symbol called the *cursor.* Usually it's a flashing line or square that indicates where text will appear when you begin typing.

When you see the Ready prompt and the cursor, you can type instructions either in *immediate mode* or as a *program.* Type almost any BASIC statement, and the computer will respond immediately; for instance, type **PRINT"X"** and press the Enter or Return key (see below), and the computer displays an **X** right away.

But if you precede that instruction with a *line number,* the computer merely memorizes it until you subsequently type **RUN** and press the Enter key. The computer then obeys that numbered instruction, and any others you have typed, in numerical order. The list of instructions is your *program;* to examine it, type **LIST** and press the Enter key.

## The Enter Key

The computer does not pay attention to anything you type until you press the Enter key (which is labeled Return on some systems). You may see text on the screen, but the computer won't "see" it until you press this key; even then, the computer will only memorize or respond to the line where the cursor is currently positioned. The label on the key may vary:

*IBM:* ↵
*Apple:* **Return**
*Commodore:* **Return**
*TRS-8Ø:* **Enter**

Note that if your computer displays 4Ø characters per line, it is easy for you to fall into the trap of thinking that you have pressed Enter when you have not. The listings in this book contain many lines that are 39 characters long. If you add an extra space in one of these lines by accident, the line will expand to the full width of your screen, so that the cursor is squeezed off the end and onto the beginning of the next line.

Seeing the cursor at the beginning of a new line may fool you into thinking that you pressed the Enter key to move it there. As a result, you may start typing the new line without having pressed Enter. The computer won't know that you completed the preceding line; it will think the new line is merely an extension of the old one, and when you do finally press Enter, it will memorize both lines as one. When you try to run the program, the computer won't be able to make sense of this double-length line and will give you a syntax-error message.

It will be difficult for you to find your error, because the double-length line will appear as two normal, separate lines on the screen. If the computer says there's a syntax error, and you can't see anything wrong, try listing only the one line in which the error is supposed to reside. For instance, if the computer says **SYNTAX ERROR IN LINE 1ØØ,** type **LIST 1ØØ** and press Enter. If the computer lists line 1ØØ *and* the line following it, you know for sure that these two lines have been joined together as one, because you forgot to divide them by pressing Enter.

The safest way to fix this kind of error is to type the two lines over again, making sure to press the Enter key at the end of each one. Try to avoid typing extra spaces that make it possible for this error to occur in the first place; if you're ever uncertain whether you pressed Enter, press it an extra time to make sure.

## Clearing the Screen

Most computers allow you to clear the screen by pressing a key or key combination.

*IBM:* **Ctrl**/key + **Home** key
*Apple:* Type the word **HOME** and press the Return key
*Commodore:* **Shift** key + **Clr/Home** key
*TRS-8Ø:* **Clear**

Note that this only erases the screen, not the program that the computer has stored in its memory.

## The Word NEW

Before you start typing a program, make sure that no other program is present in the computer's memory. There is only room for one program at a time in the computer, even though many different programs can be stored together on a disk.

To clear the computer's memory, type **NEW** and press the Enter key. This will not erase any text you see on the screen. For instance, if you list a program, then type **NEW**, you'll still see the listing on the screen. But that program has been erased in the computer's memory, which is what matters. Often, text on the screen is merely an obsolete record of your previous instructions to the computer and its previous responses.

## Interrupt

There are times when you want to stop a program while it is running. Or when you list a program, you may want to stop the listing in the middle. To do this on various computers:

*IBM:* **Ctrl** key + **Scroll Lock** key
*Apple:* **Ctrl** key + letter **C**
*Commodore:* **Run/Stop** key
*TRS-8Ø:* **Break** key

After interrupting a program, to continue running it type the word **CONT** and press the Enter key. **CONT** makes the program continue where it left off, provided you have not made any additions or alterations to the listing during the interruption.

## Pause

Instead of interrupting a listing, you can make it pause momentarily. This technique also works while a program is running, provided the program is PRINTing text at that moment.

*IBM:* **Ctrl** key + **Num Lock** key
*Apple:* **Ctrl** key + letter **S**
*Commodore:* **Ctrl** key (works with listings only)
*TRS-8Ø:* **Shift** key + @ key

To restart the program, or continue listing it, touch any other key (except on the Commodore 64 and VIC-2Ø).

## Saving and Loading Programs

When you turn off your computer, it "forgets" any program that you have typed. To make a permanent record of your program so that you can run it again in days or years to come, you must save it onto a cassette tape or floppy disk.

I don't have space to describe the various load and save commands used on different computers. Your manual probably explains this topic fairly clearly. Be sure that you know how to save a program before you start typing any of the listings in this book, and be sure that you do save any program before you try to run it. Some of the programs include POKE statements that insert data directly into computer memory, so if you make a typing error, running a program can result in the computer "hanging up" and refusing to respond to instructions that you type on the keyboard. The only way to recover from this condition is to do a system reset, or turn the computer off and then on again. Either of these operations will wipe out the computer's memory of your program. So always save a program on tape or disk *before* you try to run it.

# CHAPTER 2
# A FEW WORDS

The programs in this book rely mainly on BASIC words that work the same way on all computers. There are a few unavoidable exceptions to this rule, however—words that you may have to alter, depending on which computer you own.

I wrote the programs in 16-bit Microsoft BASIC as implemented on the IBM PC, PC*jr,* and other modern business-oriented microcomputers. If you have an IBM, Eagle, Compaq, Columbia, Zenith, or similar computer, you won't need to modify the program listings at all (except in Part 5, *Games and Graphics,* where a conversion routine is required).

If you own a Commodore, Apple, Radio Shack, or Osborne computer, you will need to make changes as follows:

### *CLS*

Apple equivalent: **HOME**
Commodore equivalent: **PRINT CHR$ (147);**
TRS-8Ø equivalent: **CLS**
Osborne equivalent: **PRINT CHR$(26);**

### *A$=INKEY$*

Apple equivalent: **GET A$**
Commodore equivalent: **GET A$**
TRS-8Ø equivalent: **A$=INKEY$**
Osborne equivalent: **A$=INKEY$**

This statement assigns a single-key input to A$. Note that the Apple II responds to this statement differently from the other computers listed—it stops and waits for a keystroke, instead of scanning the keyboard just once and continuing with the rest of the program. For this reason, a different equivalent to **A$=INKEY$** will be needed for the Apple II in some of the programs. Details will be given in the accompanying text.

### *LOCATE 1, 1*

Apple equivalent: **VTAB (1): HTAB(1)**
Commodore equivalent: **PRINT CHR$ (19);**
Radio Shack equivalent: **PRINT@Ø**
Osborne equivalent: (omit; does not exist)

### *RND(1)*

Apple equivalent: **RND(1)**
Commodore equivalent: **RND(1)**
TRS-8Ø equivalent: **RND(Ø)**
Osborne equivalent: **RND(1)**

## *PEEK and POKE on the Apple II*

Because of the unusual video memory layout on the Apple II, some of the programs in Part 5, *Games and Graphics,* must be revised for this computer where they use the word PEEK and POKE to manipulate data in the video display.

Details are given in the section headed "Converting It for Your Computer" preceding each program listing. Please be sure to read these instructions before you attempt to type any of the programs on an Apple II, II+, or IIe.

## Adapting the Programs to Suit Yourself

The preceding changes are necessary to make the programs work on your particular system. You can make other, optional changes to suit your own tastes. (Skip the rest of this chapter if you don't know much about programming.)

***Color and Sound:*** The programs in this book make no use of color or sound, because computers control these facilities in so many different ways. If your system has color or sound capability, you can check your manual to see how to add some instructions of this type and liven things up a little. My program lines are usually numbered at intervals of 1Ø or more to leave ample room for insertions.

***Lowercase Letters:*** All the listings in this book are written in uppercase (capital) letters. There are several reasons for this. First, some old-fashioned systems don't allow you to type lowercase (little) letters. Second, when a program compares text from a user's input with text stored inside the program, fewer mistakes are possible if the program and the typed text both use capital letters. Last, if you type a listing in capital letters and accidentally type a letter L instead of a numeral 1 (as many touch-typists tend to do), the mistake will be more obvious. (Remember also not to type a capital O when you are supposed to type a zero. In the listings, each zero has a diagonal line through it (Ø) to distinguish it from letter O.)

If your computer allows you to use lowercase letters and you like the way they look on the screen, by all means use them in your programs in text between quote marks following PRINT statements.

This will not affect the functioning of the programs in any way.

***REM Lines:*** When the computer finds the word **REM** at the beginning of a program line, it ignores the remainder of that line and proceeds to the next line. This allows you to type anything you like after the word **REM,** in plain English, as REMarks clarifying how the program works.

I have made full use of REM lines, to add space in the listings, divide them into sections, and explain what each section does. Since these REM lines are for your information only and are ignored by the computer, you can omit them without affecting the functioning of the programs if you want to reduce the amount of typing you do.

***Spaces:*** In the program listings, each reserved word such as PRINT, CLS, GOTO, etc., is preceded and followed by a space (or in some cases a punctuation mark). Such spaces are mandatory in modern Microsoft BASIC and make the listings easier to read. However, if your version of BASIC does not require these spaces, you can omit them. You will save a little typing and, in the case of the game programs, the statements will execute fractionally faster. On the other hand, your listings will be harder to read.

*Note:* The Apple II inserts spaces automatically in BASIC programs. As a result, when you list your program, what you see on the screen will look different from the printed version in this book. In particular, a program line of 39 characters may be processed on the Apple II so that it contains 41 or more characters and will no longer fit on one line of the 40-column video display. This will not in any way affect how well the programs work when you run them.

***Line Length:*** There are no lines longer than 39 characters in any of the listings. Longer program lines than this are permitted on almost all systems and are desirable as a way of combining statements. However, 4Ø-column video is very common on home computers, and it becomes confusing when displaying program lines containing more than 39 characters. For this reason, and to simplify the book design, I have restricted myself to short program lines even though they sometimes result in awkward logic and extra GOTOs.

If your computer displays lines containing more than 4Ø characters, you can make use of this feature to combine some of the statements I have put on separate lines. In particular, PRINT statements are easy to combine if you want to display longer pieces of text.

***Variable Names:*** Most versions of BASIC allow you to give your variables easily remembered names such as PLAYERCHOICE or SCORE. There isn't enough room in 39-character program lines for such long names, however, and long names take up more memory, which may be a consideration for readers who own very small systems.

For these reasons, variable names in this book never consist of more than two letters. Certain names are used consistently throughout:

**A, B, M,** and **N** are always loop variables, or transient variables chosen arbitrarily.
**KØ** through **K9** are always constants specified in the conversion routine that is used in Part 5, *Games and Graphics.*
**R** is always a random number.
**X** and **Y** are usually video addresses used in PEEK and POKE statements.

**A$** is usually a transient variable used in **A$=INKEY$** or **GET A$** statements.

If your computer allows long program lines and you like to use long variable names, you can easily adapt the programs to suit yourself. Just be sure that when you alter a variable, you alter *every* instance of it throughout a program.

# PART 2
# TESTS OF SKILL

# CHAPTER 3
# PREDICTOR

Can a computer predict what you're going to do next, even when you don't know yourself? It sounds unlikely, but the program listed in this chapter does exactly that, based on the principle that most people exhibit patterns that they are unaware of.

"Predictor" invites you to type a random series of ones and zeros on the computer keyboard. After 19 keystrokes, the computer starts predicting what you will type next, based on patterns that it has found in your choices so far. The longer the program runs, the better chance it has of making accurate predictions—provided, of course, that you don't consciously change your pattern of typing.

## How to Use It

As soon as you type **RUN** and press Enter, the program displays instructions and waits for you to start typing ones and zeros. Try to type them impulsively, without too much conscious thought.

To make its prediction without any possibility of trickery, the program must display it on the screen *before* you go ahead and type 1 or Ø. You can see the prediction, which may tempt you to prove the computer wrong by doing the opposite of what it predicts. To avoid this, tape a small piece of paper over just that part of the screen where the computer's prediction appears. After you have typed 1 or Ø, the display will scroll up, revealing what the prediction was.

The computer continues predicting your keystrokes for as long as you care to continue typing them. It also shows a tally of its success rate, which may fall below 5Ø percent at first, but will usually increase as the program continues.

It's important that you should not type numbers faster than the computer can process them. Otherwise, keystrokes will be lost, and the program won't be able to detect any patterns. So don't type your next number until you see the computer ask for it.

Anytime you get bored, press E to end, and the program stops and displays all the patterns of 1 and Ø that you typed. You may be surprised to find how nonrandom your choices really were. Some patterns (especially 1111 and ØØØØ) often don't appear at all; we tend to avoid typing them because they don't seem "random" enough, in our human terms. In reality, of course, a truly random series of choices should ultimately include every possible pattern.

## Adapting It for Your Computer

The word **CLS** appears on program lines 3Ø, 5ØØ, and 1Ø4Ø. The statement **A$=INKEY$** appears on lines 26Ø and 102Ø. If you're not sure whether your computer understands these words and expressions, see Chapter 2 for guidance.

If you use a TRS-8Ø, type **RND(Ø)** instead of **RND(1)** in the expression on line 22Ø.

## How It Works

I've placed this program first in the book because I think it's the most interesting, the most unusual, and the most surprising to people who doubt the ability of a little home computer to predict what they'll do next.

Unfortunately, in order to make the program predict numbers fast enough, I had to put more complicated math in it than in most of the other programs in the book. So it's not very easy to explain. Its overall strategy is simple enough, however, and it is also easy to modify, as described in the next section.

The program makes each prediction by looking at the last few digits you have typed and comparing the pattern of ones and zeros with similar patterns you have typed in the past. For instance, you may have a habit of typing a one after you have previously typed three zeros. The program checks the relative frequency of patterns of 1, 2, 3, and 4 digits to predict your next choice.

Here's a line-by-line explanation.

40–80

These lines display the playing instructions.

85

**DP** is the maximum number of digits in the patterns checked by the program. **NP** is the maximum number of patterns. **NG** is the number of computer guesses displayed so far. **CG** is the number of correct guesses. The symbol is made by pressing shift with numeral 6 on many keyboards.

90

The **PR( )** array records the number of times each pattern occurs. **CV( )** and **NV( )** are the current value and next value of the most recent **N** digits typed, expressed in coded form.

100–140

At the start of the program, no digits have been typed, so the program has no patterns to analyze. The loop **FOR M=1 TO DP** gets the user's first **DP** choices and stores them in **CV( )** and **NV( )**.

15Ø–17Ø

The next 15 choices made by the player are stored. **GOSUB 25Ø** sends the computer to the routine that asks for the player's choice, and **GOSUB 4ØØ** memorizes that choice and the resulting patterns of ones and zeros. No predictions are made yet.

18Ø

The same subroutines are called, but from earlier line numbers, so that a prediction now precedes each number typed by the player, and the computer's success rate is displayed before the program memorizes the patterns.

2ØØ–23Ø

The value of **B** has already been calculated in the the routine beginning on line 4ØØ (see below). If **B** is positive, the computer's prediction **C** is 1; otherwise, **C=Ø;** if **B=Ø,** however, **C** is assigned a random value because there are insufficient data for a prediction.

25Ø–29Ø

The program gets the next single keystroke from the keyboard, stores it in **A$,** jumps to line 500 if **A$="E",** screens out other keystrokes except for 1 or Ø, and assigns the numeric value of **A$** to **P.**

3ØØ–33Ø

The number of guesses is increased by 1, and the number of correct guesses increases if the computer's prediction has turned out to be correct. The computer's success rate is displayed as a percentage.

4ØØ–49Ø

**CV(N)** is the current value of the pattern formed by the most recent **N** digits typed, determined by considering the pattern as a binary number. The program increases by one the number of times this pattern has been observed, as recorded in **PR( ).** On line 46Ø, the pattern value is multiplied by 2 as a way of shifting the 1s and Øs one place to the left, to make room for the next digit to be typed. The result is stored in **NV(N),** the next pattern value. Lines 47Ø and 48Ø compare how many more times that value has been followed by a 1 instead of a Ø in the past. **A** is squared so that significant deviations will easily outweigh smaller variations. **B** keeps a running total as the program compares patterns of 4, 3, 2, and 1 digits.

5ØØ–64Ø
The program displays the final score.

7ØØ–92Ø
The program displays every possible combination of 1 and Ø and shows how often the user created each pattern.

1ØØØ–1Ø5Ø
This subroutine simply asks the user to press any key and waits until a key is pressed.

## Going Further

At present, the program looks for patterns involving up to 4 ones and zeros. Would it be more accurate if it checked patterns of 5 or even 6 digits? I doubt it, but you can easily find out. On line 85, instead of **DP=4,** type **DP=5** or **DP=6** to increase the maximum length of patterns that the program will inspect.

You can also see how well it does with smaller values for **DP.** The minimum is **DP=1.** This tells the program to make its predictions purely on the basis of single digits typed. If a person has typed more ones than zeros, the program predicts the next digit will be a one and vice versa. This is the most elementary form of prediction, but even this can score better than 5Ø percent.

One other modification. You could substitute a different line 28Ø:

```
28Ø A$=STR$(INT(RND(1)*2))
```

This line enables the computer to generate its own random ones and zeros, instead of having the player type them on the keyboard. The program will now try to predict its own behavior. Actually, it is checking whether the computer's random-number source is really random. Leave the program running for an hour or so, then type an E to end the run. (Apple owners will have to omit line 260 and end the run by pressing Ctrl+C, then type GOTO 500 and press the return key. The program will display the frequency of all the patterns. They should have occurred a roughly equal number of times if the RND function in your computer is properly designed.

```
10 REM                         PREDICTOR
30 CLS
40 PRINT"TYPE A RANDOM SERIES OF ONES"
50 PRINT"AND ZEROS. AFTER A WHILE,"
60 PRINT"THE COMPUTER WILL START"
70 PRINT"PREDICTING WHAT YOU WILL"
80 PRINT"TYPE NEXT.":PRINT
85 DP=4:NP=2^DP:NG=Ø:CG=Ø
9Ø DIM PR(DP,NP),CV(DP),NV(DP)
97 REM
98 REM----------------CONTROL SEQUENCE
99 REM
1ØØ FOR M=1 TO DP:GOSUB 25Ø
11Ø FOR N=DP TO 1 STEP -1
12Ø CV(N)=NV(N)+P:NEXT N
125 FOR N=DP TO 1 STEP -1
13Ø NV(N)=CV(N-1)*2:NEXT N
14Ø NEXT M
15Ø FOR M=1 TO 15
16Ø GOSUB 25Ø:GOSUB 4ØØ
17Ø NEXT M
18Ø GOSUB 2ØØ:GOSUB 3ØØ
19Ø GOTO 18Ø
197 REM
198 REM--------------PREDICTION DISPLAY
199 REM
2ØØ PRINT
21Ø C=Ø:IF B>Ø THEN C=1
22Ø IF B=Ø THEN C=INT(RND(1)*2)
23Ø PRINT"YOUR NEXT NUMBER WILL BE";C
247 REM
248 REM----------------GET PLAYER INPUT
249 REM
25Ø PRINT"TYPE 1 OR Ø (E TO END): ";
26Ø A$=INKEY$
27Ø IF A$="E" THEN 5ØØ
28Ø IF A$<>"1" AND A$<>"Ø" THEN 26Ø
29Ø PRINT A$:P=VAL(A$):RETURN
298 REM--------------------SCORE UPDATE
299 REM
3ØØ NG=NG+1
31Ø IF C=P THEN CG=CG+1
```

```
320 PRINT"% CORRECT GUESSES:";
330 PRINT INT(100*(CG/NG))
397 REM
398 REM----------------ANALYZE PATTERNS
399 REM
400 B=0:FOR N=DP TO 1 STEP -1
410 CV(N)=NV(N)+P
420 PR(N,CV(N))=PR(N,CV(N))+1
430 NEXT N
450 FOR N=DP TO 1 STEP -1
460 NV(N)=CV(N-1)*2
470 A=PR(N,NV(N)+1)-PR(N,NV(N))
480 B=B+(A*A*SGN(A))
490 NEXT N:RETURN
497 REM
498 REM----------------SHOW FINAL SCORE
499 REM
500 CLS
510 IF NG<2 THEN END
520 PRINT"BASED ON PATTERNS IT FOUND"
530 PRINT"IN YOUR 'RANDOM' SERIES OF"
540 PRINT"NUMBERS, THE COMPUTER"
550 PRINT"MADE";NG;"PREDICTIONS,"
560 PRINT"OF WHICH";CG;"WERE CORRECT."
570 PRINT:PRINT"SUCCESS RATE:";
580 PRINT INT(100*(CG/NG));
590 PRINT"PERCENT.":PRINT
600 PRINT"IF YOU HAD BET $1 PER GUESS,"
610 PRINT"YOU WOULD HAVE ";
620 A$="LOST":IF 2*CG<NG THEN A$="WON"
630 PRINT A$;ABS(2*CG-NG);"DOLLARS."
640 GOSUB 1000
698 REM---------PATTERN FREQUENCY TABLE
699 REM
700 PRINT"HERE ARE THE PATTERNS THAT"
710 PRINT"THE COMPUTER DISCOVERED:"
720 PRINT
730 DIM N$(DP+1)
800 FOR A=1 TO DP
810 FOR M=1 TO A+1:N$(M)="0":NEXT M
820 FOR N=0 TO 2^(A)-1
830 PRINT"PATTERN ";
```

```
840 FOR M=A TO 1 STEP -1
850 PRINT N$(M);:NEXT M
860 PRINT" OCCURRED";PR(A,N);"TIMES."
870 GOSUB 900:NEXT N
880 PRINT:IF A>2 THEN GOSUB 1000
890 NEXT A:END
897 REM
898 REM------UPDATE 1-0 PATTERN DISPLAY
899 REM
900 M=1
910 IF N$(M)="0"THEN N$(M)="1":RETURN
920 N$(M)="0":M=M+1:GOTO 910
997 REM
998 REM------------------ANYKEY INPUT
999 REM
1000 PRINT
1010 PRINT"PRESS ANY KEY TO CONTINUE."
1020 A$=INKEY$
1030 IF A$="" THEN 1020
1040 CLS
1050 RETURN
```

# CHAPTER 4
# TYPING TUTORIAL

Several commercially available programs claim to teach you to touch-type on your computer keyboard. These programs cost $30 or more—a considerable expense when you realize how easy it is to create such a program yourself. It won't have the fancy graphics of the commercial products, and it won't be able to save your score on disk for future reference, but it will do almost everything else.

"Typing Tutorial" displays randomly selected words on the screen, waits for you to type them, tells you how many mistakes you made, and calculates your approximate typing speed in words per minute. Unlike many other programs of this sort, it doesn't make you feel at all pressured. You work at your own pace, at whatever level you choose, for as long as you like.

## How to Use It

The program begins by asking you which level you want to try. Each of the 8 levels of difficulty makes use of more of the letters on the keyboard and longer words, involving more finger stretching from one part of the keyboard to another.

After you select a level and press Enter, the program asks how many words you want to type. You select a target for yourself, such as 1ØØ (representing 2 or 3 minutes of work for an average typist).

The program starts displaying words selected at random from its vocabulary. Each time it fills a line with words, it waits for you to type them. Then it displays a new line, and so on, until you've typed your quota.

While you are typing, no cursor is visible on the screen, and the Backspace key does not operate. Thus the program functions as much as possible like a typewriter in a typing test. If you make a mistake, you can't back up and correct it; you have to continue.

Finally, the program shows you how many words you typed, your speed in words per minute, and your net speed after deducting 2 for each mistake. Again, this is the system often used in typing tests.

## Adapting It for Your Computer

The word **CLS** appears on lines 1Ø, 1Ø5, and 31Ø. The statement **A$=INKEY$** appears on lines 22Ø and 27Ø. If your computer requires wording different from either of these expressions, check Chapter 2.

Apple users should use **GET A$** instead of **A$=INKEY$** on lines 22Ø and 27Ø.

The statement **RND(1)** occurs on line 13Ø; if you own a TRS-8Ø, you should write this as **RND(Ø)**.

On line 2Ø5Ø you'll see the expression **SW=4Ø.** If your computer displays a number of characters per line other than 4Ø, change the value of **SW** accordingly. For instance, if you have an 8Ø-character display, type

```
2Ø5Ø SW=8Ø
```

On line 2Ø6Ø, the expression **C=46ØØ** must be adjusted to make your computer estimate your typing speed with reasonable accuracy. First, type the whole program, including line 2060 as it is shown here. Then run the program and type a small number of words—40, say—while timing yourself. To figure your actual speed in words per minute, multiply the number of words by 60 and divide the result by the number of seconds you took. Compare the result with your words-per-minute score as estimated by the computer. If the computer says you typed *more* words per minute than you actually did, you need to *reduce* the value of **C** as defined on line 2060. If the computer says you typed *fewer* words per minute than you actually did, you need to *increase* the value of **C**.

Retype line 2060 and change the value of **C** by at least 100, as in **C=4700** or **C=4500.** Press Enter to tell the computer to memorize the new version of this line, then run the program again, and time yourself again. When you have adjusted the value of **C** so that the program displays your typing speed correctly to the nearest couple of words per minute, save the program and write the correct value of **C** in the listing in this book, so that you have a note of it for future use.

Note: because of the unusual way that the Apple II scans its keyboard, it is not possible for it to time your typing speed while the program is running. Apple II users should omit line 2060 and lines 340 through 410.

## How It Works

The program contains 8 lists of words in DATA statements on lines 3010 onward. Depending on which level the user selects, the program reads one of the word lists into the array **W$ ( )**, then selects words at random from this array and displays them on the screen, until one video line has been filled. The program then scans the keyboard for one keystroke at a time and displays each letter typed, noting any errors and doing a counting routine as a simple kind of clock to measure typing speed.

The most important variables are:

**SW:** Screen width, in characters per line
**NW:** Number of words the user decides to type
**TW:** Number of words typed so far
**SC:** Score (number of words typed correctly)
**TM:** Time taken so far
**C:** Converts **TM** to approximate words per minute
**LL:** Length of the line of displayed words
**LV:** Level of difficulty (1 through 8)
**WL:** Number of words in this level
**TW$** : The word currently being typed
**DW$ ( ):** Words displayed on this particular line
**W$ ( ):** The complete vocabulary of words that can be displayed at this level of difficulty.

Line by line, the program works like this:

10–95
Instructions are displayed, and the user is asked to specify **LV** (game level) and **NW** (number of words to be typed).

**100**
The program tells the computer to use subroutine **2000** to establish other variables and read the vocabulary into **W$ ( )**. See below.

120
The program adds 2 blank lines to the video display and zeros **N** (number of words displayed on the new line), **Q** (identifying number of previously displayed word), and **LL,** before displaying a new line of words.

130–140
**R** is given a random value ranging from 1 to **WL,** the total number of words at this level. If **R=Q,**

the program has chosen the same random number twice in succession, and must go back and get a new number, to avoid displaying the same word twice in succession.

150

Enough room for the new word on this video line? If not, the action jumps to line 200.

160

Word **W$ (R)** is displayed, with a space following it.

170

1 is added to the number of words on this line. The displayed word number **N** is memorized in **DW$(N).** The line length is increased by the length of the new word, plus one space following it.

180

If the program has not yet displayed the number of words specified by the user (as **NW**), the computer goes through the random word-selection cycle again.

200

The program starts a new line on the screen, and **M,** the number of words typed by the user on this new line, is zeroed.

210

The word counter, **M**, advances by 1. The typed word string is zeroed. A loop begins, to get a number of typed letters from the keyboard determined by the length of displayed word **DW$(M).**

220–240

The computer checks the keyboard. Each time it finds that no key has been pressed, 1 is added to the time counter, and the keyboard is checked again. When a key is pressed, its letter is stored in **A$** , PRINTed to the screen, and added to the end of **TW$** , which keeps a record of the word being typed

25Ø

At the end of the loop, the typed word is compared with the displayed word. If they match, the score is increased by 1.

26Ø

If the number of words typed is now equal to the number of words displayed, this line is complete, and it's time to display a new line or, if the maximum number of words has been reached, to display the score.

27Ø–29Ø

The program waits for the user to type a space between one word and the next. **TM** continues to count until the space is typed. The space appears on the screen as an asterisk, to indicate the user's position, since no cursor is displayed.

3ØØ–43Ø

The score is calculated, using **C** to convert **TM** into words per minute. If the user wants to try again, action restarts from line 3Ø.

2ØØØ–2Ø1Ø

This subroutine is executed at the beginning of each run of the program, to READ the words from the DATA statements into the **W$()** array. The DATA list is RESTOREd, and a loop begins that will READ through the intervening levels of vocabulary to the one the user wants.

2Ø2Ø

The number of words in each level, as shown in the first DATA statement in that level, is read into **WL.** The program displays periods (. . .) on the screen to show that it's still alive and working while it continues READing DATA.

2Ø3Ø

All the words in this level are read into **W$(1)** through **W$(WL).**

2Ø4Ø

If this level of vocabulary was the one selected by

the user, the **A** loop ends; otherwise, it repeats, to make the computer read the next level of vocabulary.

2Ø5Ø–21ØØ
Variables are reset, and the subroutine ends by displaying a couple of blank lines on the screen to precede the instructions.

3ØØØ–
Each level of vocabulary begins on a line number that is a multiple of 5ØØ. The first DATA statement in each level supplies the number of words in that level.

## Going Further

The most essential improvement in this program is to increase the variety of words that it displays. Otherwise, using it becomes monotonous.

I have designed it so that you can add more words easily. Check lines 35 through 55 of the program to see which letters are used in each level of difficulty. Then build your own words from those letters and add them in new lines of DATA in the appropriate sections of the vocabulary beginning on line 3ØØØ.

Very few words can be made from letters ASDFG, so I doubt you'll find anything to add to the vocabulary in Level 1. In Level 2 onward, however, there is a lot of scope for extra words.

Add as many as you like, but keep count of the total number of words in each section. Enter this new total as the number in the DATA statement at the beginning of that section. For example, if you increase Level 2 vocabulary so that it now contains 15Ø words, type **15Ø** as the item of DATA on line 35ØØ instead of the number 13 there at present. Make sure you count the number of words absolutely accurately.

Line 15 tells the computer to expect the number of

words in the **W$** array to be no more than 2ØØ. If you increase the number of words in *any one* level of the vocabulary beyond 2ØØ, you must type that number on line 15, where the number 2ØØ appears at present.

```
5 REM                          TYPING TUTORIAL
10 CLS
15 DIM W$(200), DW$(20)
20 PRINT"THIS PROGRAM HELPS YOU TO"
25 PRINT"INCREASE YOUR TYPING SPEED."
30 PRINT
35 PRINT"LEVEL 1: ASDFG"
40 PRINT"LEVEL 2: ASDFGWERT"
45 PRINT"LEVEL 3: ASDFGWERTHJKL"
50 PRINT"LEVEL 4: ASDFGWERTHJKLYUIOP"
55 PRINT"LEVEL 5: ASDFGHJKLXCVBNM"
60 PRINT
65 PRINT"LEVEL 6: ALL LETTERS, EASY"
70 PRINT"LEVEL 7: ALL LETTERS, MEDIUM"
75 PRINT"LEVEL 8: ALL LETTERS, HARD"
80 PRINT
85 INPUT"BEGIN AT WHICH LEVEL";LV
90 PRINT:PRINT"HOW MANY WORDS DO YOU ";
95 INPUT"WANT TO TYPE";NW
100 GOSUB 2000
105 CLS
110 PRINT"TYPE THESE WORDS:"
114 REM
115 REM---------DISPLAY A LINE OF WORDS
116 REM
120 PRINT:PRINT:N=0:LL=0:Q=0
130 R=INT(RND(1)*WL)+1
140 IF R=Q THEN 130
150 L=LEN(W$(R)):IF LL+L+1=>SW THEN 200
160 Q=R:PRINT W$(R);" ";
170 N=N+1:DW$(N)=W$(R):LL=LL+L+1
180 TW=TW+1:IF TW<NW THEN 130
194 REM
195 REM------------TYPE A LINE OF WORDS
196 REM
200 PRINT:M=0
210 M=M+1:TW$="":FOR A=1 TO LEN(DW$(M))
220 A$=INKEY$
230 IF A$="" THEN TM=TM+1:GOTO 220
240 PRINT A$;:TW$=TW$+A$
250 NEXT A:IF TW$=DW$(M) THEN SC=SC+1
260 IF M=N THEN 300
```

```
270 A$=INKEY$
280 IF A$<>" " THEN TM=TM+1:GOTO 270
290 PRINT"*";:GOTO 210
294 REM
295 REM-----------------CALCULATE SCORE
296 REM
300 IF TW<NW THEN 120
310 CLS
320 PRINT"OUT OF";NW;"WORDS,"
330 PRINT"YOU TYPED";SC;"CORRECTLY."
340 PRINT:PRINT"YOUR SPEED WAS";
350 A=INT((NW*C)/TM):PRINT A;
360 PRINT"WORDS PER MINUTE.":PRINT
365 IF NW=SC THEN 420
370 PRINT"LESS 2 FOR EACH MISTAKE,"
380 PRINT"YOUR NET SPEED WAS";
390 B=A-2*(NW-SC):IF B<0 THEN B=0
400 PRINT B;
410 PRINT"WORDS PER MINUTE.":PRINT
420 INPUT"TRY AGAIN";YN$
430 IF YN$<>"N" THEN 30
440 END
1994 REM
1995 REM----------------RESET VARIABLES
1996 REM
2000 PRINT:PRINT"READING DATA";
2010 RESTORE:FOR A=1 TO LV
2020 READ WL:PRINT".";
2030 FOR B=1 TO WL:READ W$(B):NEXT B
2040 NEXT A
2050 SW=40
2060 C=4600
2070 TM=0:TW=0:SC=0
2100 PRINT:PRINT:RETURN
2994 REM
2995 REM-------------LEVEL 1 VOCABULARY
3000 DATA 16
3010 DATA ADD,DAD,DADA,FAD,GAG,SAD,SAG
3020 DATA GAS,GAD,ASS,ADDS,DADS,FADS
3030 DATA GAGS,SAGS,ADDS
3494 REM
3495 REM-------------LEVEL 2 VOCABULARY
```

```
35ØØ DATA 13
351Ø DATA SAW,FAR,TAG,FAT,RAG,FED,SEA
352Ø DATA FEAR,WED,DREW,FREE,WEDS,REST
3994 REM
3995 REM--------------LEVEL 3 VOCABULARY
4ØØØ DATA 12
4Ø1Ø DATA HAS,LAD,ARK,LARK,ASK,ASH,JET
4Ø2Ø DATA JEER,LAWS,REAL,WELL,SEEK
4494 REM
4495 REM--------------LEVEL 4 VOCABULARY
45ØØ DATA 19
451Ø DATA DAY,HAY,LAY,KISS,LID,LOG,PAD
452Ø DATA JAW,SKIP,SLIP,HOOP,YELL,LADY
453Ø DATA DULL,FULL,TASK,JUT,LIP,OIL
4994 REM
4995 REM--------------LEVEL 5 VOCABULARY
5ØØØ DATA 13
5Ø1Ø DATA CAN,CAB,MAN,BAD,BAN,DAB,VAN
5Ø2Ø DATA LACK,LAX,JAM,JAB,MAX,CAM
5494 REM
5495 REM--------------LEVEL 6 VOCABULARY
55ØØ DATA 12
551Ø DATA ZOO,AXE,VEER,BIN,MOB,CON
552Ø DATA JEER,KILL,POOR,TRY,QUIP,QUIT
5994 REM
5995 REM--------------LEVEL 7 VOCABULARY
6ØØØ DATA 12
6Ø1Ø DATA EXIT,AXIOM,ZERO,VOWS,PROVE
6Ø2Ø DATA WALKED,KNITTED,OXEN,JOVIAL
6Ø3Ø DATA JINXED,FAVOR,LAZY
6494 REM
6495 REM--------------LEVEL 8 VOCABULARY
65ØØ DATA 12
651Ø DATA EXISTENTIAL,JUGGLER,DINKY
652Ø DATA WAXIEST,AVERAGED,ROUGHLY
653Ø DATA QUIZZED,ADJUNCT,GNAWING
654Ø DATA REVIVING,WRINKLES,QUIVERING
```

# CHAPTER 5
# TRAVEL QUIZ

An educational computer program should be more than a passive source of information. It should help the user along, step by step, in a responsive manner.

The program at the end of this chapter is a simple example, designed to convey some fundamental facts about U.S. geography. It invites you to imagine traveling from New York to San Francisco, passing a series of cities along the way. The names of the cities are displayed on the screen; they must be selected in the right order. Each time you make a correct choice, the computer revises the list, displaying only the names of those cities still lying ahead as your imaginary trip progresses.

The program has been designed so that you can easily adapt it to show the names of other cities, or any other items that have to be chosen in a particular sequence. You could substitute European countries, or you could display a series of tasks, such as the steps involved in turning on and using a computer. The list of items can be as short or as long as you like. More details are given in "Going Further," pp. 53–54.

## How to Use It

When you run the program, it shows you the list of 9 cities and asks you to choose the first one that you would pass if you drove from New York to San Francisco. To make your choice, type the letter identifying the city on the list, and press Enter. If your choice is wrong, you have to try again; if you're right, the program revises the list to show only the cities that still remain. You make more choices until you've worked through to the last one.

## Adapting It for Your Computer

This program is simple and requires virtually no adaptation. The only word that may vary from one computer to another is **CLS,** on lines 2Ø and 2ØØ. Check Chapter 2 if you're not sure whether your computer uses this word.

## How It Works

Here's how the program functions, line by line:

3Ø
: **NC** is the number of cities. Their names will be stored in **C$ (1)** through **C$ (NC). G** is the number of the player's next guess.

4Ø
: The names of the cities are transferred from the DATA list into the **C$ ( )** array.

5Ø–12Ø
: Instructions for using the program. Line 1ØØ displays the complete list of cities.

13Ø
: **A$** is assigned the number of the next city on the route, written as FIRST, SECOND, and so on. **B$** is assigned the letter identifying the city that should come next. Thus **B$** holds the correct answer to the question the program is about to ask.

15Ø
: The user's guess is stored in **G$** .

160
If the guess matches the correct answer, the computer skips to line 200.

210
Now that the user has typed a correct guess, the number of guesses is incremented by 1. The key letter in **B$**, identifying the city that has just been correctly chosen, is converted to a number identifying that city's position in the **C$** array. This number is assigned to **A.** The name of city **A** is replaced by letter X as a way of dropping that city from the list.

250–270
The list of cities is displayed, omitting any whose names have been chosen and replaced by an X.

280
If the number of guesses is less than the total number of cities, the trip isn't over yet, so the computer is sent back to line 130 to repeat the guessing procedure.

300–340
Since there is no point in asking the user to choose from a list in which only one city remains, the program simply displays the name of that city and ends.

## Going Further

If you want to use different city names, type them in the DATA statements on lines 1000 through 1080, in a scrambled sequence. Be sure to retain the identifying letter that precedes each name on the list; otherwise, the program won't work properly. You can type fewer names simply by leaving out lines of DATA up to and including line 1080. Or if you want a longer list, you can add more DATA lines from 1090 onward. Bear in mind that your list must be short enough to be displayable on your video screen.

On lines 1200 through 1220 you must provide the key to unscrambling your list of cities. After the word FIRST, type the identifying letter of the city that should correctly be chosen first. After the word SECOND, type the identifying letter of the city that the user should choose second; and so on. Don't leave out any commas!

If you have listed more than 9 cities, you'll have to type extra lines of DATA after 1220, in the same format, to specify the correct sequence of your extra cities. Also, if you have typed any number of cities other than 9, you must type that number instead of 9 in the statement **NC=9** on line 30.

Last, you will need to change lines 60, 70, and 330 to display text on the screen in keeping with your new choice of city names.

If you want the program to use a list of items other than cities, change the DATA statements exactly as I have already described, change the **NC=9** statement if your number of items is larger or smaller than 9, and change lines 50, 60, 70, 80, 140, 150, 230, 235, 240, 310, 320, and 330 so that appropriate instructions and commentary are displayed on the screen while the program is running. Be careful to change *only the words contained within quote marks.* You must retain any other letters and symbols, such as **;A$;** on line 140, exactly as in the original program.

```
10 REM                          TRAVEL QUIZ
20 CLS
30 NC=9:DIM C$(NC):G=1
40 FOR A=1 TO NC:READ C$(A):NEXT A
50 PRINT"WHEN YOU DRIVE FROM"
60 PRINT"NEW YORK TO SAN FRANCISCO"
70 PRINT"ALONG INTERSTATE 80"
80 PRINT"YOU PASS THESE CITIES:"
90 PRINT
100 FOR A=1 TO NC:PRINT C$(A):NEXT A
110 PRINT:PRINT"BUT NOT IN THAT ORDER."
120 PRINT:PRINT"ACTUALLY,";
130 READ A$,B$
140 PRINT"THE ";A$;" CITY YOU"
150 INPUT"PASS IS (TYPE 1 LETTER)";G$
160 IF G$=B$ THEN 200
170 PRINT:PRINT"NO, TRY AGAIN.":PRINT
180 GOTO 140
197 REM
198 REM-------------------CORRECT GUESS
199 REM
200 CLS
210 G=G+1:A=ASC(B$)-64:C$(A)="X"
220 PRINT"RIGHT! WHICH LEAVES ONLY"
230 IF G<NC THEN PRINT"THESE CITIES";
235 IF G=NC THEN PRINT"THIS CITY";
240 PRINT" STILL AHEAD OF YOU:"
250 PRINT:FOR A=1 TO NC
260 IF C$(A)<>"X" THEN PRINT C$(A)
270 NEXT A:PRINT
280 IF G<NC THEN 130
297 REM
298 REM-----------------------LAST CITY
299 REM
300 READ A$
310 PRINT"...THE ";A$;" AND LAST CITY"
320 PRINT"BEFORE YOU FINALLY REACH"
330 PRINT"SAN FRANCISCO."
340 END
```

```
998 REM-----------------LIST OF CITIES
999 REM
1000 DATA A. CHICAGO
1010 DATA B. SALT LAKE CITY
1020 DATA C. DES MOINES
1030 DATA D. RENO
1040 DATA E. SACRAMENTO
1050 DATA F. SCRANTON
1060 DATA G. OMAHA
1070 DATA H. CLEVELAND
1080 DATA I. CHEYENNE
1197 REM
1198 REM---------------CORRECT SEQUENCE
1199 REM
1200 DATA FIRST,F,SECOND,H,THIRD,A
1210 DATA FOURTH,C,FIFTH,G,SIXTH,I
1220 DATA SEVENTH,B,EIGHTH,D,NINTH,E
```

# PART 3
# WORDPLAY

# CHAPTER 6
# ORACLE

Computers were originally developed to do mathematical calculations. Within a few years, however, it became apparent that computer programs could shuffle words almost as easily as numbers. Since then, much research has been done into artificial intelligence: programs that make a computer respond to the user in a way that seems almost human, even though the computer itself doesn't really "understand" human language.

A high-level artificial intelligence program would be too long to list and explain here, but shorter programs use the same general principles, and this part of the book offers three examples. Although they are designed as games appealing primarily to young computer users, they can easily be developed into demonstrations that seem eerily intelligent.

"Oracle," listed in this chapter, invites you to type any question beginning with WHO, WHAT, WHEN, WHERE, or WHY. The program gives you an answer that often makes surprisingly good sense. Type, WHO AM I? and the program may well reply, A SLY AND SNEAKY HUMAN BEING. Type, WHERE DO I LIVE? and the program may respond, A SLEAZY GHETTO NEIGHBORHOOD. The program does not understand your questions or its own responses. It is merely shuffling words according to a set of very simple rules, which I will explain later.

## How to Use It

When you run the program and type in your question, if it does not begin with WHO, WHAT, WHEN, WHERE, or WHY, the program will refuse to accept it.

The computer will "think" for a moment before supplying an answer. You can then ask another question and carry on a whole dialogue. This is particularly impressive to people who know nothing about computers and are willing to believe that it really comprehends what they type on the keyboard. To sustain this illusion, it's best not to let anyone use the program for very long; it will slip up and give a meaningless answer or begin to repeat itself. By restricting your friends to a couple of questions each, you'll preserve the mystique of your pet "electronic brain."

## Adapting It for Your Computer

**CLS** on line 3Ø, **A$=INKEY$** on line 28Ø, and **RND(1)** on lines 22Ø and 24Ø may need to be altered to suit your particular computer. See Chapter 2. Commodore owners should type lines 11Ø and 15Ø like this:

```
110 IF B$="WHO"+CHR$(32) THEN Q=1
150 IF B$="WHY"+CHR$(32) THEN Q=5
```

## How It Works

There are two ways to design a program that will give appropriate answers to open-ended questions. First, you can trust to luck and compile a lot of vague, mysterious statements to be selected by the computer totally at random, without any reference to what the user has actually typed on the keyboard.

The *I Ching* works this way. For example, it once advised me, "Do not make your journey across the great water," the day before I was due to make a transatlantic flight. This appropriate answer sticks in my mind years after I have forgotten all the other dumb answers the *I Ching* ever gave me, much as a mystic's single correct prediction tends to be remembered while all his numerous blunders are forgotten.

A totally random program, then, can sometimes seem oddly clairvoyant . . . but only sometimes.

A better approach is to get the program to *analyze* the user's question for keywords or phrases, then choose a preprogrammed answer that is more likely to fit. A famous program of this kind was "Doctor," written by Joseph Weizenbaum in 1966 at MIT. When the user typed problems on the computer keyboard, the program supplied responses such as, ARE YOU SAYING 'NO' JUST TO BE NEGATIVE? or, TELL ME MORE ABOUT YOUR FAMILY.

Analyzing a user's statements thoroughly enough to give such specific answers would have been too complex for this book, so I've designed "Oracle" to give only five types of responses, depending on whether the user's question begins with WHO, WHAT, WHEN, WHERE, or WHY. In each category, the computer chooses its random answer from 1Ø possible sentences, so that it won't seem to repeat itself too much when consulted several times in succession.

The program is not complicated, and works like this:

4Ø–9Ø

Instructions are displayed, and the user's question is stored in **Q$.** If the question contains more than 5 letters, execution skips to line 1ØØ; otherwise, the program complains that it wasn't asked a proper question and loops back to line 4Ø.

1ØØ–15Ø

The leftmost 4 letters of the question are stored in **B$**, then compared against keywords on lines 11Ø through 15Ø. This is known as "parsing a sentence"—finding out what it means.

16Ø–19Ø

Line 1ØØ gave **Q** an initial value of Ø. Lines 11Ø through 15Ø altered that value if the program "recognized" the first word of the question. Line 16Ø reasons that if **Q** is now greater than Ø, a match must have been found, so the computer can skip to line 2ØØ; otherwise, the user must not have typed WHO, WHAT, WHEN, WHERE, or WHY, in which case execution loops back to line 6Ø.

2ØØ–23Ø

The **RND** function will be used to select an answer. **RND** always begins with the same sequence of numbers when the computer is switched on, so it's best to sample it an arbitrary number of times before using its output. Lines 21Ø through 23Ø sample **RND** a number of times equal to the length of the user's question.

24Ø–25Ø

**R** is assigned an integer ranging from Ø through 9. The loop READs DATA a number of times determined by **1Ø*Q**, less the value of **R**. Each new line of DATA is stored in **A$**, displacing the one that was there before. At the end of the loop, **A$** contains the final random statement drawn from the section of DATA appropriate to the value of **Q**.

26Ø–28Ø

The statement is displayed as the "answer" to the question. A period is added at the end of it. The user is given the option of rerunning the program.

1ØØØ–5ØØ9

Answers to the various categories of questions.

## Going Further

This program is particularly easy to modify. First, you can substitute your own answers in any of the DATA statements. Keep them as vague and general as possible, like the advice in newspaper astrology columns. Avoid using a comma in any of your answers; it will be interpreted as a terminator dividing the single sentence into two pieces of DATA. If you must use punctuation, you'll have to enclose the sentence in quote marks to tell the computer it's all one piece of DATA.

You can add more answers to each section on extra lines of DATA. Each section must always contain the same number of lines of DATA as all the other sections, and where the number 1Ø crops up on lines 24Ø and 25Ø, you must type the new number of answers in each section instead.

You can also change the program to allow the user to begin each question with a wider choice of words. There are only so many ways of asking a question in English; it is quite possible to write a program that checks for all of them. If a question begins with WAS, WERE, or DID, for instance, the program can supply some sort of answer in the past tense. A question beginning with WILL would be about the future, so the computer can make a prediction. If the user's question also contains the word *I,* the user is probably asking about his or her own future, which will enable the program to give a highly specific answer.

To search for a particular sequence of letters within a string (in this case, letter *I* preceded and followed by a space) use the INSTR function if your version of BASIC has it, or use a loop to examine middle parts of the string 3 letters at a time, with a MID$ function.

A sneaky way of making the program seem highly

intelligent is to compile a list of questions that people commonly ask, such as WHO AM I? or WHAT TIME IS IT? Then add 10 or 20 lines to the program, checking to see whether the user has typed one of these specific, common questions. If so, the program can display a specific, preset answer. The extra program lines would look something like this:

```
151 IF Q$="WHO AM I?" THEN 400

400 A$="A HUMAN BEING, STUPID.":GOTO 260
```

You could also add the ability to memorize the most recent questions, so that the computer can give an insulting response if the user asks the same thing twice. The possibilities are limited only by the size of your computer memory—and ultimately by the number of ways in which the computer can examine each question, within a reasonable amount of time.

```
10 REM                          THE ORACLE
30 CLS
40 PRINT"TYPE ANY QUESTION BEGINNING"
50 PRINT"WHO, WHAT, WHEN, WHERE, WHY:"
60 PRINT:INPUT"  ";Q$:PRINT
70 IF LEN(Q$)>5 THEN 100
80 PRINT"THAT'S NOT A QUESTION!":PRINT
90 GOTO 40
97 REM
98 REM-----------------EXAMINE QUESTION
99 REM
100 B$=LEFT$(Q$,4):Q=0
110 IF B$="WHO "THEN Q=1
120 IF B$="WHAT"THEN Q=2
130 IF B$="WHEN"THEN Q=3
140 IF B$="WHER"THEN Q=4
150 IF B$="WHY "THEN Q=5
160 IF Q>0 THEN 200
170 PRINT"YOUR QUESTION HAS TO BEGIN"
```

```
180 PRINT"WITH WHO, WHAT, WHEN, WHERE,"
190 PRINT"OR WHY. TRY AGAIN:":GOTO 60
197 REM
198 REM-------------------FIND AN ANSWER
199 REM
200 PRINT"MY ANSWER IS..."
210 FOR N=1 TO LEN(Q$)
220 R=RND(1)
230 NEXT
240 R=INT(RND(1)*10)
250 FOR N=1 TO (10*Q)-R:READ A$:NEXT
260 PRINT A$;".":PRINT
270 PRINT"ASK ME ANOTHER?"
280 A$=INKEY$
290 IF A$="N" THEN END
300 IF A$="Y" THEN RESTORE:GOTO 40
310 GOTO 280
997 REM
998 REM-------------------ANSWERS TO WHO
999 REM
1000 DATA A WELL-KNOWN CATHOLIC SAINT
1001 DATA A DOWNTRODDEN PEASANT
1002 DATA A SLY AND SNEAKY HUMAN BEING
1003 DATA A RELIGIOUS FANATIC
1004 DATA A CERTIFIABLE MORON
1005 DATA AN OBNOXIOUS MENTAL DEFECTIVE
1006 DATA THE WRONG SORT OF PERSON
1007 DATA A TOTAL HUMAN FAILURE
1008 DATA A NOTORIOUS PARTY BORE
1009 DATA A GENIUS SURROUNDED BY NERDS
1997 REM
1998 REM-----------------ANSWERS TO WHAT
1999 REM
2000 DATA UNMANAGEABLE AND INTIMIDATING
2001 DATA HIDDEN IN YOUR GUILTY PAST
2002 DATA THE ANSWER TO ALL YOUR DREAMS
2003 DATA OPPOSITE OF WHAT YOU EXPECT
2004 DATA LATER THAN YOU THINK
2005 DATA A TOTAL WASTE OF YOUR DAY
2006 DATA WHAT INDEED!
2007 DATA WHATEVER YOU REALLY WANT
2008 DATA NOTHING FOR A COMPUTER TO SAY
```

```
2009 DATA THIS YOU REALLY DO NOT NEED
2997 REM
2998 REM----------------ANSWERS TO WHEN
2999 REM
3000 DATA BEFORE THE END OF THE CENTURY
3001 DATA USUALLY LAST THING AT NIGHT
3002 DATA AT A MOMENT OF GREAT BOREDOM
3003 DATA DURING A TIME OF DESPERATION
3004 DATA AT A TIME OF PEACEFUL ENNUI
3005 DATA SHORTLY BEFORE MIDDAY E.S.T.
3006 DATA PROBABLY DURING LUNCH
3007 DATA IN AN ELECTION YEAR
3008 DATA DURING COLLECTIVE INSANITY
3009 DATA AFTER AN AGE OF GREAT STRIFE
3997 REM
3998 REM---------------ANSWERS TO WHERE
3999 REM
4000 DATA A SLEAZY GHETTO NEIGHBORHOOD
4001 DATA A LITTLE HOUSE ON THE PRAIRIE
4002 DATA A FOUL-SMELLING PUBLIC TOILET
4003 DATA UNDER THE BED
4004 DATA WEST OF YOUR PRESENT LOCATION
4005 DATA NOWHERE SAFE OR SALUBRIOUS
4006 DATA IN A TOUGH WATERFRONT SALOON
4007 DATA IN AN EXOTIC FAR-OFF COUNTRY
4008 DATA ACROSS THE GREAT OCEAN
4009 DATA A PLACE FEARED BY SANE MEN
4997 REM
4998 REM-----------------ANSWERS TO WHY
4999 REM
5000 DATA FOR REASONS KNOWN ONLY TO GOD
5001 DATA GIVE ME ONE REASON WHY NOT
5002 DATA TO GET TO THE OTHER SIDE
5003 DATA TO FOSTER BETTER HEALTH
5004 DATA HUMAN NATURE IS VERY PERVERSE
5005 DATA WE BOW TO AMBITION AND GREED
5006 DATA PEOPLE ARE SIMPLY LIKE THAT
5007 DATA STUPIDITY AND INCOMPETENCE
5008 DATA THERE IS NO RATIONAL REASON
5009 DATA FEW PEOPLE ARE AT ALL PERFECT
```

# CHAPTER 7
# GUESS THE NAME

Here's a guessing game to amuse young computer users. One person types a 5-letter name; another then tries to guess it. The program offers 3 clues, then reveals the secret word.

This program is useful for demonstrating the use of subroutines and string manipulation in BASIC—two techniques that beginning programmers often find confusing.

## How to Use It

The second player has to guess the secret word typed by the first player, so the second player shouldn't be allowed to see the screen while the first part of the program is running.

The first person enters the secret name on the keyboard one letter at a time. The screen then clears, and the second player takes over, trying to guess the name. The computer provides 3 clues: the first, last, and middle letter.

Readers who want a more challenging word-guessing game should take a look at "Adult Hangman" in Chapter 16.

## Adapting It for Your Computer

If your computer does not understand the word **CLS,** check Chapter 2 to find out which word to use on lines 2Ø and 2ØØ of the program.

## How It Works

Here's the precise function of each group of lines in the program:

3Ø–8Ø
: Two blocks of instructions are displayed, separated by two lines of space.

1ØØ–14Ø
: The word FIRST is stored in **X$.** Execution skips to line 1ØØØ (see p. 69). Execution returns and transfers the first letter of the name from **L$** to **A$.** This cycle is repeated for the second through fifth letters of the name, which are stored in **B$** through **E$.**

15Ø
: All 5 letters are assembled and stored as the complete name in **N$.** They were obtained from the player one at a time because they will be used individually in the next part of the program. The program would have been shorter if it obtained the name all at once, then broke it into single letters with a MID$ function, but I wanted it to be as simple as possible, involving no math and a minimum of BASIC vocabulary.

2ØØ–3ØØ
: Three hints are displayed: the first, fifth, and middle letter of the secret name. After each hint, execution skips to subroutine 2ØØØ (see p. 69), which gets the second player's guess and stores it in **G$** . If this matches the name in **N$** , the player wins; otherwise, execution returns from subroutine 2ØØØ and the program displays the next hint.

1000–1050

The program asks for each letter in the name separately, identifying them via the words FIRST, SECOND, etc., stored in **X$** . Any character outside of the alphabet is rejected. Any input longer than 1 character is rejected.

2000–2100

The second player is asked to guess the name. The guess is stored in **G$** . If it is correct, the subroutine (and the program) terminates; otherwise, the subroutine returns execution from where it came, earlier in the program.

## Going Further

The technique of asking for a word one letter at a time, then showing sample letters as a hint to help a second player guess the word, could be used on a larger scale with longer words or names. The letters could be displayed jumbled, as an anagram. A time limit could be introduced. A version could be written that would store two secret words, one typed by each player, and would then allow each player to take turns at guessing. This would be a similar game to Jotto, the old pencil-and-paper game in which two players try to guess each other's words on the basis of clues about individual letters in the words. Adapting Jotto as a two-player game to run on a computer would be relatively easy; adapting it as a game between one player and the computer would be infinitely more difficult because the computer would have to make guesses based on a full knowledge of the English language. A complete dictionary of 5-letter words would be stored on disk; BASIC would not be fast enough for consulting such a large reference source, and it is well outside the scope of amateur programming.

```
10 REM                        GUESS THE NAME
20 CLS
30 PRINT"ONE PERSON TYPES A NAME."
40 PRINT"THE OTHER TRIES TO GUESS IT."
50 PRINT:PRINT
60 PRINT"IT MUST BE A 5-LETTER NAME."
70 PRINT"TYPE THE LETTERS 1-AT-A-TIME."
80 PRINT:PRINT
100 X$="FIRST":GOSUB 1000:A$=L$
110 X$="SECOND":GOSUB 1000:B$=L$
120 X$="THIRD":GOSUB 1000:C$=L$
130 X$="FOURTH":GOSUB 1000:D$=L$
140 X$="LAST":GOSUB 1000:E$=L$
150 N$=A$+B$+C$+D$+E$
197 REM
198 REM-----------------CLUES & GUESSES
200 CLS
210 PRINT"HINT: THE FIRST LETTER IN ";
220 PRINT"THE NAME IS ";A$:GOSUB 2000
230 PRINT"HINT: THE LAST LETTER IN ";
240 PRINT"THE NAME IS ";E$:GOSUB 2000
250 PRINT"THE MIDDLE LETTER IS ";C$
260 GOSUB 2000
270 PRINT"YOU DIDN'T GUESS IT."
280 PRINT"THE NAME WAS ";N$
300 END
997 REM
998 REM------------SINGLE-LETTER INPUTS
999 REM
1000 PRINT"THE ";X$;" LETTER ";
1010 INPUT"IN THE NAME IS";L$
1020 IF L$<"A" OR L$>"Z" THEN 1000
1030 IF LEN(L$)=1 THEN PRINT:RETURN
1040 PRINT:PRINT"ONE LETTER ONLY!"
1050 PRINT:GOTO 1000
1997 REM
1998 REM--------------WHOLE-NAME INPUTS
1999 REM
2000 PRINT
```

```
2010 INPUT"WHAT'S THE SECRET NAME";G$
2020 PRINT:IF G$=N$ THEN 2100
2030 PRINT"WRONG!":PRINT:RETURN
2100 PRINT"RIGHT! YOU WIN.":END
```

# CHAPTER 8
# INTERACTIVE STORY

Usually, you have a passive role when you read; you are not allowed any opportunity to "interact" with a short story or a novel. It has one beginning, one ending, one plot connecting the two, and no way of changing it if it doesn't happen to appeal to you.

Interactive fiction, however, allows you a series of choices, so that you skip through different sections of the story to a variety of different endings. For example, if the hero has to choose between battling a strange alien creature or jumping in a spaceship and blasting off to safety, you decide which is the most sensible option and skip to an appropriate section later in the book.

Adventure games for computers work on a similar principle. In fact, interactive fiction is really better suited to a computer than to a book. This chapter's program is an example: a multiple-choice saga chronicling the misadventures of an exiled extraterrestrial stranded on Earth. Disguised as a young woman, her aim is to understand everyday life and find the "American Dream." The reader's job is to guide her through to this happy ending, which isn't easy; there are four endings, only one of which is happy, and the chances of reaching it are 3 in 25, or 12 percent.

Typically, a full-length interactive-story program would be as long as this whole book. To reduce the concept to just 6 pages, I had to make some compromises, abbreviating the descriptions and dialogue and using a minimum number of episodes. The program is long enough to allow 25 different paths through the plot, however, and if you're a good typist, you can easily expand the text to flesh out some of the descriptions and add personal touches of your own.

## How to Use It

When you run the program, it displays text describing the opening scene of the story and two options for continuing from there. Type 1 or 2, press Enter, and the next episode appears on the screen. You continue selecting options until you reach one of the endings.

## Adapting It for Your Computer

**CLS,** on lines 2Ø and 5Ø2Ø, is the only word you may need to change to make the program run on your system. Check Chapter 2 if you're not sure.

## How It Works

The program is longer than most others in this book, but its logic is extremely simple. The listing consists mainly of PRINT statements to display text on the screen.

The listing has been divided into sections that all follow the same format. Each section begins on a line number that is a multiple of 1ØØ (except for the opening section, on lines 2Ø through 18Ø). After displaying text, the program does a **GOSUB 5ØØØ** to get the reader's choice of options, which is stored in **C.** The value of **C** is then used to branch to the next section of the program, which repeats the sequence.

Sections K, L, and N are unhappy endings that allow no further options; the computer is told to **GOTO 4000,** where a "you lose!" message is displayed and the user is offered the option of playing again.

Section O is the happy ending and is also the end of the program.

Because many of the lines in this program are 39 characters long, take special care to press Enter after you type each one. If you accidentally add a space in a line, forcing the cursor down to the next line on the screen, you may be fooled into thinking you've pressed Enter when you really haven't. This pitfall is discussed in more detail in the section of Chapter 1 dealing with the Enter key.

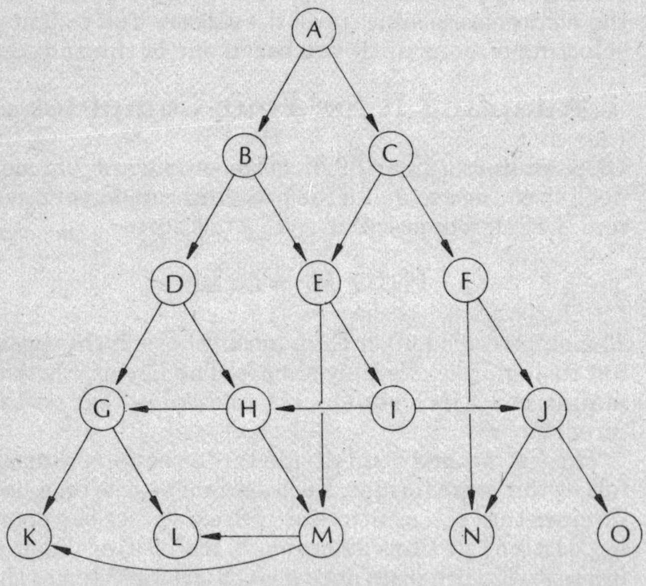


Links between the sections of the interactive story are indicated by arrows in this diagram. 25 different plot-paths are possible. Of the four endings, section O is the only happy one. Since there are only three possible paths from section A to section O, the reader's chances of reaching the happy ending are 3 in 25, or 12%.

## Going Further

Looking at the program listing, it's hard to visualize exactly how the GOTO statements connect each story section to the next. A plot diagram makes the structure clearer. Each arrow represents a GOTO statement that in turn represents a possible path through the plot of the story.

You can enhance this interactive story in several ways. First, you can insert extra PRINT statements to expand the descriptive text and add some touches of your own. If your computer displays lines longer than 40 characters, you can also extend the PRINT lines that already exist. Provided the GOTOs remain the same, the structure of the program won't be affected.

Second, you can extend the story beyond the endings that I have written. Sections K, L, N, and O, the current endings, can be replaced with new choices, branching to extra sections that you write yourself on new lines 1600 through 3900.

Before you attempt this, draw your own copy of the plot diagram on a very large sheet of paper, so you have room to write notes about what happens in each section. You can now trace the various paths through the plot and invent your own continuation. After you have penciled new sections onto the bottom of the diagram, type them into the program; run the program repeatedly to make sure your new plot paths work properly under all circumstances.

Once you've done this, you'll have some idea of how to write an interactive story of your own.

You can also adapt this program so that when someone uses it, the episodes of the story are printed out onto paper. This way, the user has a permanent record of his or her path through the story. Check your computer manual if you are not sure how to modify the word PRINT so that it sends text to your printer instead of to the screen. Different versions of BASIC do this in different ways.

```
10 REM                    INTERACTIVE STORY
20 CLS
30 PRINT"IN THIS STORY, YOU DECIDE HOW"
40 PRINT"THE PLOT PROGRESSES. YOUR AIM"
50 PRINT"IS TO REACH THE HAPPY ENDING."
60 PRINT
70 PRINT"THIS IS THE SAGA OF MELANIE"
80 PRINT"MUTANT, AN ALIEN BEING EXILED"
90 PRINT"FROM HER HOME PLANET. SHE"
100 PRINT"MUST SPEND THE REST OF HER"
110 PRINT"LIFE DISGUISED AS AN EARTH"
120 PRINT"WOMAN HIDING AMONG US.":PRINT
124 REM
125 REM-----------------------SECTION A
126 REM
130 PRINT"FINDING HERSELF IN THE USA,"
140 PRINT"SHE RESOLVES TO PURSUE THE"
150 PRINT"AMERICAN DREAM. SHOULD SHE"
160 PRINT
170 PRINT"1:SETTLE IN SUBURBIA"
180 PRINT"2:TRY LIFE IN THE BIG CITY"
190 GOSUB 5000:ON C GOTO 200,300
194 REM
195 REM-----------------------SECTION B
196 REM
200 PRINT"AFTER SCANNING THE SUBURBAN"
210 PRINT"WANT ADS, MELANIE DECIDED"
220 PRINT
230 PRINT"1:TO WORK AS A WAITRESS AT"
240 PRINT"  THE INTERNATIONAL HOUSE OF"
250 PRINT"  PANCAKES IN A LOCAL MALL"
255 PRINT
260 PRINT"2:TO BECOME AN AVON LADY"
290 GOSUB 5000:ON C GOTO 400,500
294 REM
```

```
295 REM-----------------------SECTION C
296 REM
300 PRINT"AFTER SEARCHING ALL OVER"
310 PRINT"TOWN, MELANIE GOT A JOB"
320 PRINT
330 PRINT"1:SERVING CUSTOMERS IN AN"
340 PRINT"  EXCLUSIVE DEPARTMENT STORE"
345 PRINT
350 PRINT"2:AS A CAB DRIVER"
390 GOSUB 5000:ON C GOTO 500,600
394 REM
395 REM-----------------------SECTION D
396 REM
400 PRINT"WORKING AT IHOP WAS TOUGH"
410 PRINT"FOR A SENSITIVE YOUNG THING"
420 PRINT"FROM OUTER SPACE! STILL"
430 PRINT"TANTALIZED BY THE AMERICAN"
440 PRINT"DREAM, MELANIE DECIDED TO"
445 PRINT
450 PRINT"1:MARRY THE PANCAKE CHEF"
455 PRINT
460 PRINT"2:RUN OFF WITH ONE OF HER"
465 PRINT"  CUSTOMERS, A MYSTERIOUS"
470 PRINT"  MAN NAMED BOB, WHO CLAIMED"
475 PRINT"  HE COULD MAKE HER RICH!"
490 GOSUB 5000:ON C GOTO 700,800
494 REM
495 REM-----------------------SECTION E
496 REM
500 PRINT"PANDERING TO THE TASTES OF"
510 PRINT"FEMALE EARTH BEINGS WAS VERY"
520 PRINT"DIFFICULT FOR MELANIE. BUT"
530 PRINT"THEN ONE OF HER CUSTOMERS,"
540 PRINT"JOAN, INVITED HER TO"
545 PRINT
550 PRINT"1:VISIT HER ECCENTRIC"
555 PRINT"  MILLIONAIRE BROTHER, BOB"
560 PRINT
570 PRINT"2:GET RICH QUICK SELLING"
575 PRINT"  COUNTERFEIT TUPPERWARE"
580 PRINT"  SMUGGLED IN FROM TAIWAN"
590 GOSUB 5000:ON C GOTO 900,1300
```

```
595 REM------------------------SECTION F
596 REM
600 PRINT"DRIVING A CAB WAS EASY FOR A"
610 PRINT"GIRL USED TO DRIVING UFO'S!"
620 PRINT"BUT ONE NIGHT MELANIE WAS"
630 PRINT"ROBBED AT GUNPOINT BY A GUY"
640 PRINT"CALLING HIMSELF 'BADASS BOB.'
650 PRINT"IN DESPERATION, SHE"
655 PRINT
660 PRINT"1:PUNCHED HIM IN THE JAW"
665 PRINT
670 PRINT"2:SURRENDERED HER MONEY AND"
675 PRINT"  TAXI AND TOLD HIM, 'THIS"
680 PRINT"  IS ALL I OWN. TAKE IT!"
690 GOSUB 5000:ON C GOTO 1000,1400
694 REM
695 REM------------------------SECTION G
696 REM
700 PRINT"ALAS, HER NEW HUSBAND TURNED"
710 PRINT"OUT TO BE HORRIBLY BORING."
720 PRINT"MELANIE THOUGHT WISTFULLY"
730 PRINT"OF LIFE BACK AT THE CRAB"
740 PRINT"NEBULA, WHERE THERE WERE 11"
745 PRINT"DIFFERENT SEXES. BUT SHE WAS"
750 PRINT"STUCK ON EARTH, SO SHE"
755 PRINT
760 PRINT"1:WROTE A BOOK ABOUT HERSELF"
770 PRINT
775 PRINT"2:STARTED HANGING OUT AT"
780 PRINT"  SLEAZY DISCOTHEQUES"
790 GOSUB 5000:ON C GOTO 1100,1200
794 REM
795 REM------------------------SECTION H
796 REM
800 PRINT"BOB OWNED A COLONIAL MANSION"
810 PRINT"WITH BIG FRONT DOORS AND 4"
820 PRINT"PILLARS OUT FRONT. STUNNED,"
825 PRINT"SHE AGREED TO MARRY HIM! BUT"
830 PRINT"THEN HE CONFESSED THE SOURCE"
840 PRINT"OF HIS VAST WEALTH. HE WAS"
850 PRINT
860 PRINT"1:A COMPUTER PROGRAMMER"
```

```
870 PRINT
880 PRINT"2:A WHOLESALE DOPE DEALER"
890 GOSUB 5000:ON C GOTO 700,1300
894 REM
895 REM----------------------SECTION I
896 REM
900 PRINT"WHILE JOAN BARBECUED SOME"
910 PRINT"BURGERS, BOB AND MELANIE GOT"
920 PRINT"DRUNK ON DAIQUIRIS IN THE"
930 PRINT"DEN. 'SUDDENLY I FEEL I LOVE"
940 PRINT"YOU!' BOB EXCLAIMED, HUGGING"
950 PRINT"MELANIE WILDLY. SHOCKED, SHE"
955 PRINT
960 PRINT"1:CONFESSED SHE FELT THE"
965 PRINT"  SAME WAY ABOUT HIM"
970 PRINT
975 PRINT"2:PUNCHED HIM IN THE JAW"
990 GOSUB 5000:ON C GOTO 800,1000
994 REM
995 REM----------------------SECTION J
996 REM
1000 PRINT"ENRAGED BY HER PUNCHING HIM"
1010 PRINT"OUT, BOB SUED FOR ASSAULT"
1020 PRINT"--AND WON! MELANIE SPENT 30"
1030 PRINT"DAYS IN JAIL. BY THE TIME"
1040 PRINT"SHE WAS PAROLED, SHE HAD"
1050 PRINT
1060 PRINT"1:VOWED TO DEVOTE HER LIFE"
1065 PRINT"  TO HELPING THE URBAN POOR"
1070 PRINT
1075 PRINT"2:DISCOVERED GOD"
1090 GOSUB 5000:ON C GOTO 1400,1500
1095 REM--------------------SECTION K
1096 REM
1100 PRINT"WHEN MELANIE'S BOOK WAS"
1110 PRINT"PUBLISHED, IT WAS A TOTAL"
1120 PRINT"FAILURE. NO ONE BELIEVED A"
1130 PRINT"WORD OF IT. SHE RESIGNED"
1140 PRINT"HERSELF TO LIVING OUT THE"
1150 PRINT"REST OF HER 340-YEAR LIFE"
1160 PRINT"SPAN IN TOTAL DEPRESSION."
1180 GOTO 4000
```

```
1194 REM
1195 REM-----------------------SECTION L
1196 REM
1200 PRINT"LIFE AT THE DISCO GAVE"
1210 PRINT"MELANIE HEARING DAMAGE AND"
1220 PRINT"MIGRAINES. AND COCAINE"
1230 PRINT"INTERACTED WITH HER ALIEN"
1240 PRINT"METABOLISM TO TURN HER SKIN"
1250 PRINT"PERMANENTLY BLUE! IN A FIT"
1260 PRINT"OF DESPAIR, SHE OVERDOSED"
1270 PRINT"UNDER THE BIG ROTATING BALL"
1280 PRINT"COVERED IN LITTLE MIRRORS."
1290 GOTO 4000
1294 REM
1295 REM-----------------------SECTION M
1296 REM
1300 PRINT"MELANIE WAS SOON RAKING IN"
1310 PRINT"CASH FROM DEALING HER COM-"
1320 PRINT"PANION'S IMPORTED PRODUCT!"
1330 PRINT"SHE DECIDED TO RETIRE AND"
1340 PRINT
1350 PRINT"1:WRITE HER LIFE STORY"
1360 PRINT
1370 PRINT"2:JOIN THE FASHIONABLE SET"
1380 PRINT"  AT THE DISCOTHEQUE"
1390 GOSUB 5000:ON C GOTO 1100,1200
1394 REM
1395 REM-----------------------SECTION N
1396 REM
1400 PRINT"ALAS, LIFE IS NO PICNIC IN"
1410 PRINT"THE URBAN JUNGLE! MELANIE"
1420 PRINT"GAVE ALL SHE HAD, BUT IT"
1430 PRINT"WASN'T ENOUGH TO COMPENSATE"
1440 PRINT"FOR HER WHITE-MIDDLE-CLASS"
1450 PRINT"ELITISM--EVEN THOUGH SHE"
1460 PRINT"PROTESTED SHE WAS A VISITNG"
1470 PRINT"ALIEN LIFE FORM WHO UNDER-"
1480 PRINT"STOOD OPPRESSED MINORITIES."
1490 PRINT"SHE WAS FOUND DEAD IN A"
1492 PRINT"FIREBOMBED TENEMENT."
1493 GOTO 4000
1494 REM
```

```
1495 REM-----------------------SECTION O
1496 REM
1500 PRINT"MELANIE ESTABLISHED THE"
1510 PRINT"CHURCH OF THE BELOVED CRAB"
1520 PRINT"NEBULA. IT WAS AN INSTANT"
1530 PRINT"SUCCESS! SOON SHE WAS DOING"
1540 PRINT"TV APPEALS, AND $$$ WERE"
1550 PRINT"ROLLING IN. SHE HAD FOUND"
1560 PRINT"THE AMERICAN DREAM, JUST AS"
1570 PRINT"SHE HAD IMAGINED IT.":PRINT
1580 PRINT"THE END."
1590 END
3994 REM
3995 REM----------------------TRY AGAIN?
3996 REM
4000 PRINT
4010 PRINT"TOO BAD! YOU DIDN'T GUIDE"
4020 PRINT"MELANIE THROUGH TO THE"
4030 PRINT"AMERICAN DREAM.":PRINT
4040 INPUT"DO YOU WANT TO TRY AGAIN";Y$
4050 IF Y$="N" THEN END
4060 RUN
4994 REM
4995 REM--------------1 OR 2 SUBROUTINE
4996 REM
5000 PRINT:INPUT"YOUR CHOICE";C
5010 IF C<1 OR C>2 THEN 5000
5020 CLS
5030 RETURN
```

# PART 4
# FACTS AND FIGURES

# CHAPTER 9
# PHONE WORDS

The programs in this part of the book supply you with various types of information that could not be conveyed so usefully in any other medium.

"Phone Words," in this chapter, helps you remember telephone numbers by turning them into words. You type the phone number into the computer, and it displays all the permutations of letters corresponding with that sequence of digits on the telephone dial. (By the word *dial* I mean touch-tone buttons as well as old-fashioned rotary dials.) Buried somewhere in all the different permutations is usually a "phone word" that spells out something appropriate and is much more memorable than its numeric equivalent.

## How to Use It

When you run the program, it asks you to type the phone number you want to remember. A local phone number of 7 digits will yield up to 2187 phone words, which take about 4 minutes to be displayed by the computer. A number of 1Ø digits, including the area code, can generate nearly 6Ø,ØØØ letter permutations, which the computer takes nearly *2 hours* to display. You'd have a lot of work to do, searching through that many "words" for one that makes some kind of sense.

You can type the phone number with or without a hyphen or space separating groups of digits. When you press the Enter key, the computer pauses for a moment, then displays the phone words for your inspection.

One problem about finding letter combinations to match a phone number is that no letters appear beside the numbers 1 and Ø on a U.S. telephone. This program compromises by assigning letter Z to number Ø, and letter Q to number 1, since these two letters aren't used elsewhere on the dial. You could also assign letter O to numeral Ø, instead of placing it with M and N beside number 6 on the dial. All you need to do is make a simple change in the DATA statements in the program; see "Going Further," p. 89.

## Adapting It for Your Computer

**CLS,** on line 5ØØ, is the only BASIC word in this program that varies from one computer to another. Check Chapter 2 if you're not sure whether your system uses this word.

## How It Works

Because I wanted the display routine to run as fast as possible, I gave all the active lines in the program that display the phone words on the screen low line numbers at the beginning of the listing. The program contains a few GOTO statements, which the computer obeys more quickly when they are followed by low line numbers. The computer needs less time to convert a low number into its own binary numbering system, and less time to find that line if it is near the beginning of the program.

With the display routine placed first, the instructions and setup follow on line 5ØØ onward as one big subroutine. **GOSUB 5ØØ** on line 2 tells the computer to go and obey that subroutine; the computer returns to line 3, which is where the display of the phone words begins. It ends on line 8.

The most important variables include:

**N$** : Phone number typed by the user
**RN$** : Revised phone number, after eliminating punctuation
**D$( )**: Stores groups of phone letters copied from DATA
**PL$ ( )**: Stores phone letters matching each digit in **RN$**
**N( )**: Stores the number of phone letters in each of the groups corresponding with each of the digits in the phone number. Most groups contain three phone letters (e.g., ABC, corresponding with number 2 on the dial)
**C( )**: Counts the letter displayed in each group
**NP:** Number of permutations displayed so far

The logic of the program is complex, but, line by line, it works like this:

500–550
Instructions are displayed. User's phone number is stored in **N$** .

610
Groups of phone letters are transferred from DATA into **D$(1)** through **D$(10)** for easy subsequent reference.

620–650
The phone number in **N$** is examined one character at a time. Any characters other than numerals are thrown out, and the remaining digits are assembled in **RN$.**

810
The program now examines each digit in **RN$** and assigns its value to **V.**

83Ø

The counter for each group of phone letters is set to 1. The number of letters in each group is established.

84Ø–86Ø

The **B** loop, inside the **A** loop, assigns each phone letter individually to **PL$.** This way, **PL$(1,1)** through **PL$(1,3)** are the three phone letters corresponding to the first digit in the user's phone number; **PL$(2,1)** through **PL$(2,3)** are the three phone letters corresponding to the second digit; and so on. It will now be easier and faster for the program to select and display these letters.

3

This **A** loop PRINTs one letter for each digit in the phone number. The letters are selected by the value of **C(A),** the counter that keeps track of which letter was last displayed in each group.

4

The comma after PRINT starts a new column on the screen. **B** is set to the length of the phone number; it will now be used to select each counter in turn, as **C(B).**

5

Counter number **B** is advanced by 1. If the counter has not gone beyond **N(B),** the number of letters in this phone-letter group, the computer skips back to line 3 to display another phone word, different by one letter from the previous word.

6–8

If counter **C(B)** has reached its limit, it is reset to 1, and, provided **B**  **Ø,** the next counter is incremented and another phone word is displayed. If all the counters have advanced to their limits, all the letters in all the groups have been displayed as phone words, so the program displays the number of permutations and ends.

# Going Further

The most useful improvement in this program would be to direct its output to a printer instead of to the video screen. To do this, different computers adapt the word PRINT in different ways. On the IBM PC, for instance, you need only substitute **LPRINT** for **PRINT**.

You will probably have to revise line 4 so that it sends a line feed to your printer after generating enough phone words to fill one line. Check your computer manual for further details.

The letters that are used to construct phone words are stored as DATA in lines 9ØØ through 93Ø. I added spaces before Q and Z simply so that the layout looks like a touch-tone phone. The spaces are ignored when the letters are read by the program into **D$ (1)** through **D$ (1Ø)**.

If you alter the distribution of letters among the groups —for instance, by shifting O down beside Z so that they both correspond to number Ø on the dial— more usable phone words will be generated as a result. You'll have to remember that letter O now corresponds with numeral Ø, not 6.

```
1 REM                         PHONE WORDS
2 GOSUB 5ØØ
3 FOR A=1 TO L:PRINT PL$(A,C(A));
4 NEXT A:PRINT,:B=L:NP=NP+1
5 C(B)=C(B)+1:IF C(B)<=N(B) THEN 3
6 C(B)=1:B=B-1:IF B>Ø THEN 5
7 PRINT:PRINT:PRINT NP;"PERMUTATIONS."
8 END
497 REM
498 REM----------------------INSTRUCTIONS
499 REM
5ØØ CLS
51Ø PRINT"THIS PROGRAM DISPLAYS ALL OF"
```

```
520 PRINT"THE LETTER PERMUTATIONS THAT"
530 PRINT"CORRESPOND TO THE DIGITS"
540 PRINT"IN A TELEPHONE NUMBER.":PRINT
550 INPUT"WHAT'S THE NUMBER";N$:PRINT
597 REM
598 REM-----------------SET VARS; SCAN #
599 REM
600 RN$="":NP=0:L=LEN(N$):DIM D$(10)
610 FOR A=1 TO 10:READ D$(A):NEXT A
620 FOR A=1 TO L:A$=MID$(N$,A,1)
630 IF A$<"0" OR A$>"9" THEN 650
640 RN$=RN$+A$
650 NEXT A:L=LEN(RN$)
797 REM
798 REM------------ASSIGN LETTER EQUIVS
799 REM
800 DIM PL$(L,3),C(L),N(L)
810 FOR A=1 TO L:V=VAL(MID$(RN$,A,1))
820 IF V=0 THEN V=10
830 C(A)=1:N(A)=LEN(D$(V))
840 FOR B=1 TO N(A)
850 PL$(A,B)=MID$(D$(V),B,1)
860 NEXT B:NEXT A:RETURN
897 REM
898 REM---------------TOUCH-TONE LAYOUT
899 REM
900 DATA   Q,ABC,DEF
910 DATA GHI,JKL,MNO
920 DATA PRS,TUV,WXY
930 DATA      Z
```

# CHAPTER 10
# TINY DATA BASE

Data bases come in many different shapes and sizes. On-line data bases store specialized information that can only be accessed via telephone lines. Data-base programs sold for business use are able not only to store information but also to sort it, pass it to word processors or spreadsheets, and manipulate it mathematically. Much smaller programs, such as the one at the end of this chapter, store and retrieve limited amounts of personal information such as entries in an address book.

All these systems have one principle in common. A computer memory, or memory device such as disk or tape, is used like an old-fashioned file cabinet as a place to store useful facts. The computer is then programmed to help the user retrieve facts by searching for keywords.

For instance, an on-line data base that stores medical journals would allow you to retrieve every article in which a keyword such as *coronary* or *diabetes* appeared. The ability of computers to search and compare in this way, at very high speed, is the main advantage of a data base over an old-fashioned filing system. In addition, a data base of your own enables you to edit, delete, and add entries flexibly, produce various alphabetical listings, and print selected entries in various formats, ranging from business letters to address labels.

"Tiny Data Base" incorporates these features as much as is possible within a small BASIC program. I have set it up to work as an address book, including space for phone numbers and a few other items that you can choose for yourself. You can type new entries, search the entries in a variety of ways, display an alphabetical listing, and alter the displayed format. Because this program is designed to be as simple as possible, it doesn't perform all the functions of a commercial system and isn't quite as convenient to use. It is practical for files of up to 1ØØ names and addresses, though, and can be easily adapted to store other kinds of data if you wish.

## How to Use It

The program is "menu driven," which means it displays a "menu" of options from which you select, by number, the one that you want.

The first menu offers only two options: list all the entries alphabetically or find an entry. Whichever option you go for, you are then asked to choose which line the program should use to select entries. Suppose you choose line 2, family name. If you want an alphabetical listing, the program will sequence the entries alphabetically by family name. Or if you are searching for one entry, you type the family name as your "search string," or keyword.

Suppose you can't remember the person's family name. In that case, you tell the computer to select entries by first name, or city, or any other line you like.

You don't even have to type the whole name. If you tell the computer to search for an entry whose family name is D, it will find and display every entry with a family name of D *or longer*—that is, all entries beginning with D. Or ask it to search for every entry with a phone number of 415, and it will display all entries with San Francisco phone numbers. Thus you can do partial listings—of everyone in a certain city, or with a certain zip code, or whatever you like.

Different computers adapt the word **PRINT** in different ways to send text to a printer instead of to the video screen. I have not attempted to tabulate all these different systems, so "Tiny Data Base" is set up to display text on a video screen only. Your computer manual should tell you how to print BASIC text onto paper. On the IBM PC, for instance, you simply use the word **LPRINT** instead of **PRINT**.

"Tiny Data Base" naturally allows you to add new entries and edit old ones. This option isn't included on the menu displayed by the program because to add or alter entries, you have to list the program instead of running it. Different computers store data on disk or tape in so many different formats that it was impossible to generalize this program to work with tape or disk systems. So I designed it to store its entries as lines of DATA, within the program itself, from line 2ØØØ onward.

I've included four sample entries to show you the necessary style. This style *must* be followed carefully. When you replace the sample entries and add new ones of your own, follow these rules.

1. Each program line number (starting with line 2ØØØ) that is a multiple of 1Ø is a REM line, to separate one entry from the next.
2. Number the next 6 lines at intervals of 1 to avoid confusion. The first of these lines shows first and family names, separated by a comma. This comma is essential. If a person has two or more first names, list them both before the comma. If this entry is for a business, without the name of a person, type an X for the first name, then a comma, then the business name. Alternatively, you can put the business name

on the second line of DATA; the advantage of putting the business name where a family name would normally be is that when you do an alphabetical listing by family name, the business entries will be included in sequence.

3. The third line of data is for the street address. The fourth line is for town, state, and zip; they *must* be separated by commas. The fifth line is for the phone number. The sixth line is for any two other items of data that are useful; as I've set it up, one item is for the "salutation" name (the formal or informal name you use when you greet this person in a letter), and the other item is the person's spouse's name. The use of the sixth line is explained in "Going Further."
4. Two important rules: First, because commas are used to separate one item from the next on some DATA lines, do not use a comma within any single data item. Instead of IBM, INC you must type IBM INC. Second, if you lack an item of data to type in its appropriate space, you *must* type an X instead. Otherwise, the computer's DATA count will be wrong. So if you don't know a person's phone number, or you don't want to use a salutation name, type an X instead.
5. To edit an entry that you previously typed, simply list the program and edit those DATA lines, then save the program back onto disk or tape. To delete an entry, either delete all its lines or use an X instead of each piece of missing data. Remember to type X twice on the first and sixth lines, with a comma between the two X's; and type X 3 times on the fourth line of the entry, to substitute for the missing city, state, and zip.

Following this format is a hassle, but it simplifies programming a great deal. If the data were stored on disk, you would have to start dealing with file structure, input and output commands, and more.

As I have set it up, all the entries are typed in capital letters. If you want to use upper- and lowercase instead, by all means do so, but remember that when you run the program and search for an entry, you will have to type your search string in exactly the same style as the entry. To a small computer, letter **A** and letter **a** are not the same at all, so it won't find a match between the two.

## Adapting It for Your Computer

The only word you may need to change to suit your system is **CLS,** which appears on lines 2Ø, 1ØØ, 22Ø, and 6ØØ. Check Chapter 2 if you're not sure whether your computer understands this word.

## How It Works

The data base carries out two basic operations: searching for an entry by reading through its lines of DATA, and displaying those lines on the screen. Because DATA are read from the top of the program down, the word RESTORE is needed to start at the beginning of the list in each search. Because the user will not necessarily search for the first item in each entry, once an entry has been found, the DATA list must be RESTOREd all over again, and scanned again from the beginning, to reach the first item in the entry concerned. This takes time and is the major defect of the program, but there's no way around it on most systems.

All the main operations are written as subroutines so that they can be carried out in any sequence by putting together a series of GOSUB statements. Line by line, it works like this:

30

**GOSUB 1900** establishes the main variables that will be used in the program. This is not strictly necessary but is useful to avoid confusion. A line of dashes is stored in **L$** and will be used to create layouts.

40–90

The main menu is displayed. Variable A is assigned the number of options in the menu. **GOSUB 500** refers to a subroutine that asks the user to choose an option between 1 and **A.** The choice number is stored in **C,** which is then used to branch to line **100** or line **200**.

110

**GOSUB 600** calls a subroutine that asks the user to choose the line of each entry that the computer should use in alphabetizing the entries. **L** is assigned this line number. **P$,** which holds the previous entry examined, is assigned an exclamation point (!) because, in the computer's code system, ! comes before **A** in the alphabet (and before all punctuation, numerals, etc.).

120

**GOSUB 800** refers to a subroutine that finds the next entry in the alphabet after the previous entry, **P$** (see 800). If all entries have been displayed, **E** will have a value of 0; otherwise, it will give the entry number.

130

**GOSUB 300** calls a subroutine that displays entry number **E.** Then **GOSUB 1200** is used to find any subsequent entries that share the same line **L** as the one just displayed. Several people may share a name such as SMITH, for instance.

140

If a same-name entry has been found, the computer is sent back to line 130 to display it.

150

The current entry name now becomes the previous entry name, assigned to **P$.** The computer cycles back to line 120 to display the next alphabetical entry.

200

This program section controls the finding of an entry. **GOSUB 600** asks the user to select entry line **L,** as before; then the user has to type the search string, which is assigned to **S$.**

210–230

**GOSUB 1200** is used to find any entries whose first **S** letters match **S$.** If no match is found, the computer will read through to the asterisks marking the end of the data list, in which case the search ENDs.

240

If an entry is found, it is displayed (using subroutine 300), and the computer is sent back to line 220 to see if any other entries also match **S$.**

300–490

To reach entry number **E,** the computer has to read through the 10 items in each intervening entry. The rest of this routine controls the layout of displayed items in the chosen entry. To adjust the layout, see "Going Further," pp. 98–99.

800–870

To find the next entry in the alphabet, search string **S$** is assigned ZZZ. Each time an entry is found preceding the value of **S$,** the entry's text on line **L** is assigned to **S$,** provided it is subsequent to **P$,** the previously displayed entry. Entries where line **L** is missing and has been replaced with an X are skipped. When the routine reads through to the asterisks, all the data have been scanned.

1200–1250

This routine selects the next entry. If the entry isn't the line of asterisks marking the end of the data, the routine reads through to line **L** in the entry, then compares the first **S** letters of it with **S$**, the search string. If a match is found, the routine ends; otherwise, it loops back and moves to the next entry.

## Going Further

When you replace the sample lines of DATA in the listing with your own lines and add extra lines, remember to follow the format described in "How to Use It." Do not leave out or alter the 1Ø asterisks separated by commas on line 5ØØØØ. Do not type any DATA lines after that line.

Lines 32Ø through 41Ø control the format in which the items of an entry are displayed. The **PRINT** at the end of lines 33Ø, 34Ø, 35Ø, etc., tells the computer that the next item of data should appear on a new video line. If, instead, you want all the items on the same line, separated by commas (for instance), substitute **PRINT",";** instead of **PRINT** on the affected program lines. If you want some of the items not to be displayed at all, leave out the PRINT instructions for those items—but keep all the **GOSUB 48Ø** instructions. **GOSUB 48Ø** must appear 1Ø times to make the program read through all 1Ø items in the entry. Whether you PRINT those items, and in what format, is up to you.

To adapt this program for storing other kinds of data, all you need to do is use a different list of classifications on lines 63Ø through 72Ø. For instance, if you don't want to include the Salutation Name or Spouse Name, type some other heading(s) here, and substitute different kinds of data in your entries.

The purpose of Salutation Name and Spouse Name is to allow this program to be adapted to generate personalized form letters. Such a letter should begin by retrieving the recipient's address, then typing

DEAR at the beginning and inserting the name by which you usually greet the person concerned. Later in the letter, it may be useful to insert another personalized touch, by inquiring about the recipient's wife or husband. All you do is type something like GIVE MY BEST WISHES TO (Spouse Name) and get the program to insert the relevant name.

See if you can figure out how to add a form-letter generator on lines 1300 through 1890, which are available for this purpose. You can make form letters a new option, number 3 on the main menu, which will cause program execution to jump to line 1300. Then use a series of GOSUBs similar to those on lines 200 through 240 to select the recipient(s) of the letter. Use a version of subroutine 300 to display the name and address. Use PRINT statements to create the text of the letter. And READ and PRINT the personalized items of data where they are appropriate.

```
10 REM                            TINY DATA BASE
20 CLS
30 GOSUB 1900:PRINT L$
40 PRINT"           TINY DATA BASE"
50 PRINT L$:PRINT
60 PRINT"1:LIST ENTRIES ALPHABETICALLY"
70 PRINT
80 PRINT"         2:FIND AN ENTRY"
90 A=2:GOSUB 500:IF C=2 THEN 200
97 REM
98 REM-------------------------CHOICE 1
99 REM
100 CLS
110 GOSUB 600:P$="↓"
120 GOSUB 800:IF E=0 THEN END
130 GOSUB 300:GOSUB 1200
```

```
140 IF X$<>"*" THEN 130
150 P$=S$:GOTO 120
197 REM
198 REM-----------------------CHOICE 2
199 REM
200 GOSUB 600:INPUT"SEARCH STRING";S$
210 RESTORE:E=0:S=LEN(S$)
220 CLS
230 GOSUB 1200:IF X$="*" THEN END
240 GOSUB 300:GOTO 220
297 REM
298 REM------------------SHOW AN ENTRY
299 REM
300 RESTORE:IF E=1 THEN 320
310 FOR A=1 TO 10*(E-1):READ X$:NEXT A
320 GOSUB 480:IF X$<>"X" THEN PRINT" ";
330 GOSUB 480:IF X$<>"X" THEN PRINT
340 GOSUB 480:IF X$<>"X" THEN PRINT
350 GOSUB 480:IF X$<>"X" THEN PRINT
360 GOSUB 480:PRINT", ";
370 GOSUB 480:PRINT"     ";
380 GOSUB 480:PRINT:PRINT
390 PRINT" PHONE: ";:GOSUB 480:PRINT
400 PRINT"  DEAR: ";:GOSUB 480:PRINT
410 PRINT"SPOUSE: ";:GOSUB 480:PRINT
420 PRINT L$:INPUT"NEXT";X$:PRINT L$
430 RETURN
450 REM-----
480 READ X$:IF X$<>"X" THEN PRINT X$;
490 RETURN
497 REM
498 REM--------------GET USER'S CHOICE
499 REM
500 PRINT:PRINT L$:INPUT"YOUR CHOICE";C
510 IF C<1 OR C>A THEN 500
520 PRINT L$:RETURN
597 REM
598 REM--------------SELECT ENTRY LINE
599 REM
600 CLS
610 PRINT L$
620 PRINT"SELECT ENTRIES BY:":PRINT
```

```
630 PRINT"1. FIRST NAME"
640 PRINT"2. FAMILY NAME"
650 PRINT"3. BUSINESS NAME"
660 PRINT"4. STREET ADDRESS"
670 PRINT"5. CITY NAME"
680 PRINT"6. STATE"
690 PRINT"7. ZIP CODE"
700 PRINT"8. PHONE NUMBER"
710 PRINT"9. SALUTATION NAME"
720 PRINT"10. SPOUSE NAME"
730 A=10:GOSUB 500:L=C:RETURN
797 REM
798 REM-----------------FIND NEXT ENTRY
799 REM
800 RESTORE:S$="ZZZ":N=0:E=0
810 N=N+1:FOR A=1 TO L:READ X$:NEXT A
820 IF X$="*" THEN RETURN
830 IF X$="X" THEN 860
840 IF X$<S$ AND X$>P$ THEN S$=X$:E=N
850 IF L=10 THEN 810
860 FOR A=L+1 TO 10:READ X$:NEXT A
870 GOTO 810
1197 REM
1198 REM------------FIND MATCHING ENTRY
1199 REM
1200 E=E+1:FOR A=1 TO L:READ X$:NEXT A
1210 IF X$="*" THEN RETURN
1220 IF S$=LEFT$(X$,S) THEN RETURN
1230 IF L=10 THEN 1200
1240 FOR A=L+1 TO 10:READ X$:NEXT A
1250 GOTO 1200
1897 REM
1898 REM------------ESTABLISH VARIABLES
1899 REM
1900 A=0:C=0:E=0:L=0:N=0:S=0
1910 P$="":S$="":X$=""
1920 L$="-----------------------------"
1930 RETURN
1997 REM
2000 REM--------------NAMES & ADDRESSES
2001 DATA JOHN,SMITH
2002 DATA X
```

```
2003 DATA 123 ANYSTREET
2004 DATA ANYTOWN,PA,18942
2005 DATA 202 123 4567
2006 DATA JACK,MARY
2010 REM-----
2011 DATA X,BIG COMPUTERS INC.
2012 DATA SILICON HOUSE
2013 DATA SILICON PLAZA
2014 DATA SILICON CITY,CA,91234
2015 DATA 213 111 0000
2016 DATA SIRS,X
2020 REM-----
2021 DATA ZELDA SUE,VAN PELT
2022 DATA MAMIE'S MASSAGE PARLOR
2023 DATA 999 THE STRIP
2024 DATA SIN CITY,NEVADA,X
2025 DATA X
2026 DATA HONEYPIE,X
2030 REM-----
2031 DATA HENRY,JONES
2032 DATA IMPECUNIOUS CORP.
2033 DATA 11 CHAPTER STREET
2034 DATA DEBTVILLE,CA,94112
2035 DATA 213 555 7890
2036 DATA HENRY,X
2040 REM-----
50000 DATA *,*,*,*,*,*,*,*,*,*
```

# CHAPTER 11
# ANXIETY PROFILE

The test-yourself quiz at the end of this chapter is designed to be fun and informative at the same time. You answer a series of questions; the program scores your answers according to a built-in formula; it develops a "personality profile" that shows how good you are at coping with aspects of everyday life that commonly make people anxious.

The test is adapted from one used for psychological evaluation at a New York college. This is not to say that its results are foolproof or 100 percent reliable; indeed, many people challenge the validity of any tests of this type. On the other hand, I've found that most people who use it agree that it sums them up fairly accurately; you can entertain yourself comparing your test results with those of your friends—to discover who's most freaked out by modern life.

## How to Use It

When you run the program, it displays instructions and waits for you to press any key to begin. The program then displays a series of 85 common causes of anxiety and asks you to estimate how much each one bothers you by typing 1, 2, or 3. After the 85th question, the program shows your anxieties tabulated in 10 broad categories. The degree of anxiety is indicated by the length of a line of equal signs (=) in bar-chart form, and also by an equivalent percentage figure.

If you want your chart printed on paper instead of displayed on the video screen, the program's PRINT statements will have to be altered; see "Going Further," pp. 1Ø6–1Ø7.

When you have typed the program, you must give it a test run in case there are errors in your listing that would make the results inaccurate. Run the program and type a 3 in response to *every* question. You should then see an anxiety profile that rates each category 1ØØ percent. If any category shows more or less than 1ØØ percent, you made an error in one of your DATA statements on lines 8Ø1, 8Ø3, 8Ø5, etc. Check the numbers on these lines carefully.

If your anxiety profile displays fewer than 1Ø categories and ends with an OUT OF DATA or similar error message, you must have omitted one or more lines of DATA in your listing.

## Adapting It for Your Computer

The word **CLS** appears on lines 2Ø, 11Ø, and 3ØØ, and **A$=INKEY$** appears on lines 9Ø and 22Ø. If your computer doesn't understand either of these statements, check Chapter 2 to find an appropriate substitute.

The expression **LOCATE 1,1** appears on lines 14Ø and 25Ø to home the cursor without clearing the screen. Some substitute statements are listed in Chapter 2, but on a few computers, such as the Osborne 1, no substitute is possible. If this is the case on your system, omit line 14Ø and lines 25Ø through 27Ø completely. The program won't display its text as neatly, but will still run.

## How It Works

A list of 85 common causes of anxiety appears in DATA statements beginning on line 800. Following each worry is a DATA line of three figures, telling the program which anxiety categories to increase, and how much to increase them, if the user admits to having this particular concern.

For instance, following the first fear, BEING IN A STRANGE PLACE, the figures 1, 4, and 9 tell the computer to increase anxiety categories 4 and 9 by 1 point if the user is "slightly nervous" about being in a strange place, or by double this amount if the user is "more than slightly nervous." The list of anxiety categories appears on DATA lines 971 through 980.

At the end of the test, the program displays the list of categories, along with the figure that has accumulated in each, expressed as a percentage—100 percent being the maximum possible score.

Line by line, it works like this:

115–120
After displaying instructions, the program establishes its variables. **SP$** is a string of 36 spaces. **AX(1)** through **AX(10)** will store the cumulative score in each anxiety category, 1 through 10.

130–170
A loop begins that displays each question in turn, starting at the top of the screen each time. **SP$** is used to erase any part of the previous question that remains on the screen because the wording of the current question is shorter.

180–240
The program gets the user's choice. **V** is assigned 0, 1, or 2 when the user types 1, 2, or 3, respectively.

250–270
A prompt mark (>) is displayed beside whichever option the user has just chosen.

280–290
The score in the affected anxiety category is increased, and a delay loop makes the computer count from 1 to 100 so there is a momentary pause before the main loop displays the next question.

310–340
Each anxiety category is displayed; if the score in that category is greater than zero, a proportionate number of "=" marks is PRINTed on the screen.

350–400
The score is displayed as a percentage in each category. Finally, a verdict is displayed at the bottom of the screen, and the user is given the option of rerunning the program.

## Going Further

If you want a permanent record of your test results printed on paper, all of the PRINT statements on lines 300 through 400 must be adapted so that they tell the computer to send text to your printer instead of to the screen. On the IBM PC and similar systems, you type **LPRINT** instead of **PRINT** to accomplish this. On other computers, the command varies. Check your instruction manual for details.

When the program displays the scores in bar-chart form, you may be able to improve the look of the chart by substituting a different character for the "=" mark in the **PRINT"=";** statement on line 340. Use another character of your choice—ideally a graphics character, if your system has them. Instead of **PRINT"=";** try typing **PRINT CHR$(N);** where **N** is a number from 129 upward. You should be able to produce a solid bar, like a real bar chart, with the right character code.

If your screen displays more than 4Ø characters per line, you can further improve the look of the chart. Where the expression **PRINT A$;":"** appears on line 32Ø, type **PRINT A$;":";TAB(18);** instead. This will put each bar of the bar chart on the same line as the name of its anxiety category.

Other modifications of this program must be cosmetic only (e.g., different screen layouts or colors). The logic cannot be changed without upsetting how the anxiety profile is scored.

```
1Ø REM                         ANXIETY PROFILE
2Ø CLS
3Ø PRINT"THIS PROGRAM ASKS EIGHTY-FIVE"
4Ø PRINT"QUESTIONS ABOUT THINGS THAT"
5Ø PRINT"MAKE YOU NERVOUS. IT SHOWS"
6Ø PRINT"THE RESULTS TABULATED AS"
7Ø PRINT"TEN CATEGORIES OF ANXIETY."
8Ø PRINT:PRINT"PRESS ANY KEY TO BEGIN."
9Ø A$=INKEY$
1ØØ IF A$="" THEN 9Ø
11Ø CLS
115 FOR N=1 TO 12:SP$=SP$+"   ":NEXT N
12Ø DIM AX(1Ø)
127 REM
128 REM---------------DISPLAY QUESTIONS
129 REM
13Ø FOR N=1 TO 85:READ A$,A,B,C
14Ø LOCATE 1,1
145 PRINT"QUESTION NUMBER";N:PRINT
15Ø PRINT"DO YOU GET AT ALL"
16Ø PRINT"TENSE OR NERVOUS ABOUT:"
17Ø PRINT:PRINT A$;"?";
175 PRINT LEFT$(SP$,4Ø-POS(X)):PRINT
18Ø PRINT" 1:NOT AT ALL"
19Ø PRINT" 2:SLIGHTLY"
2ØØ PRINT" 3:MORE THAN SLIGHTLY"
21Ø PRINT:PRINT"TYPE 1, 2, OR 3"
22Ø A$=INKEY$
23Ø IF A$="" THEN 22Ø
24Ø V=VAL(A$)-1:IF V<Ø OR V>2 THEN 22Ø
```

```
250 LOCATE 1,1
260 FOR M=1 TO 7+V:PRINT:NEXT M
270 PRINT">"
280 AX(B)=AX(B)+V*A:AX(C)=AX(C)+V*A
290 FOR M=1 TO 100:NEXT M:NEXT N
297 REM
298 REM--------------------DISPLAY SCORE
299 REM
300 CLS
310 PRINT"YOUR ANXIETY PROFILE:":PRINT
320 FOR N=1 TO 10:READ A$:PRINT A$;":"
330 PRINT"   ";:IF AX(N)=0 THEN 350
340 FOR M=1 TO AX(N):PRINT"=";:NEXT M
350 PRINT TAB(33);INT((AX(N)*10)/3);"%"
360 NEXT N
370 PRINT"30% IS AN AVERAGE ";
380 PRINT"SCORE; 60% IS HIGH."
390 INPUT"ANOTHER PROFILE (Y/N)";A$
400 IF A$="Y" THEN RUN
410 END
797 REM
798 REM---------------------ANXIETY LIST
799 REM
800 DATA BEING IN A STRANGE PLACE
801 DATA 1,4,9
802 DATA THE NOISE OF VACUUM CLEANERS
803 DATA 2,10,0
804 DATA THE SIGHT OF AN OPEN WOUND
805 DATA 1,2,0
806 DATA BEING ALONE
807 DATA 3,4,0
808 DATA LOUD VOICES
809 DATA 1,7,0
810 DATA DESCRIPTIONS OF DEAD PEOPLE
811 DATA 1,1,0
812 DATA SPEAKING IN PUBLIC
813 DATA 1,5,6
814 DATA CROSSING BUSY STREETS
815 DATA 1,9,10
816 DATA PEOPLE WHO SEEM INSANE
817 DATA 1,2,0
818 DATA THE POSSIBILITY OF FALLING
```

```
819 DATA 2,3,Ø
82Ø DATA AUTOMOBILES
821 DATA 2,3,1Ø
822 DATA BEING TEASED
823 DATA 1,5,7
824 DATA VISITING THE DENTIST
825 DATA 1,3,7
826 DATA THUNDER
827 DATA 1,4,9
828 DATA POLICE OR AMBULANCE SIRENS
829 DATA 1,1Ø,Ø
83Ø DATA FAILURE
831 DATA 1,6,Ø
832 DATA ENTERING ROOM OF SEATED PEOPLE
833 DATA 1,5,Ø
834 DATA HIGH PLACES ON LAND
835 DATA 1,4,9
836 DATA THE VIEW FROM HIGH BUILDINGS
837 DATA 1,3,9
838 DATA WORMS
839 DATA 1,8,Ø
84Ø DATA IMAGINARY CREATURES
841 DATA 2,8,Ø
842 DATA DEALING WITH STRANGERS
843 DATA 1,5,Ø
844 DATA RECEIVING INJECTIONS
845 DATA 1,2,3
846 DATA BATS
847 DATA 1,8,Ø
848 DATA JOURNEYS BY TRAIN
849 DATA 2,3,1Ø
85Ø DATA JOURNEYS BY BUS
851 DATA 2,3,1Ø
852 DATA JOURNEYS BY CAR
853 DATA 2,3,Ø
854 DATA FEELING ANGRY
855 DATA 1,6,7
856 DATA PEOPLE IN AUTHORITY
857 DATA 1,6,7
858 DATA FLYING INSECTS
859 DATA 1,8,Ø
86Ø DATA SUDDEN NOISES
```

```
861 DATA 1,9,Ø
862 DATA DULL DREARY WEATHER
863 DATA 1,9,Ø
864 DATA LARGE CROWDS
865 DATA 1,3,Ø
866 DATA WIDE-OPEN SPACES
867 DATA 2,4,Ø
868 DATA CATS
869 DATA 1,8,Ø
87Ø DATA ONE PERSON BULLYING ANOTHER
871 DATA 1,7,Ø
872 DATA TOUGH-LOOKING PEOPLE
873 DATA 1,7,Ø
874 DATA LARGE BIRDS
875 DATA 1,8,Ø
876 DATA BEING NEAR DEEP WATER
877 DATA 1,9,Ø
878 DATA BEING WATCHED WHILE WORKING
879 DATA 1,6,Ø
88Ø DATA DEAD ANIMALS
881 DATA 3,1,8
882 DATA WEAPONS
883 DATA 2,7,1Ø
884 DATA DIRT
885 DATA 1,2,Ø
886 DATA CRAWLING INSECTS
887 DATA 1,8,Ø
888 DATA THE SIGHT OF PEOPLE FIGHTING
889 DATA 1,7,Ø
89Ø DATA UGLY PEOPLE
891 DATA 1,2,6
892 DATA FIRE
893 DATA 1,9,Ø
894 DATA SICK OR DISEASED PEOPLE
895 DATA 1,2,Ø
896 DATA DOGS
897 DATA 1,8,Ø
898 DATA BEING CRITICIZED
899 DATA 1,5,6
9ØØ DATA SEEING STRANGE SHAPES
9Ø1 DATA 1,9,Ø
9Ø2 DATA RIDING IN ELEVATORS
```

```
903 DATA 1,9,10
904 DATA SEEING A SURGICAL OPERATION
905 DATA 1,1,2
906 DATA ANGRY PEOPLE
907 DATA 1,7,0
908 DATA MICE
909 DATA 1,8,0
910 DATA THE SIGHT OF BLOOD
911 DATA 1,2,0
912 DATA PARTING FROM FRIENDS
913 DATA 2,4,0
914 DATA ENCLOSED PLACES
915 DATA 1,1,9
916 DATA THE PROSPECT OF SURGERY
917 DATA 1,1,2
918 DATA FEELING REJECTED BY OTHERS
919 DATA 3,4,5
920 DATA RIDING IN AIRPLANES
921 DATA 1,9,10
922 DATA MEDICAL ODORS
923 DATA 1,1,2
924 DATA BEING DISAPPROVED OF BY OTHERS
925 DATA 1,5,6
926 DATA NONPOISONOUS SNAKES
927 DATA 1,8,0
928 DATA GRAVEYARDS
929 DATA 3,1,0
930 DATA BEING IGNORED
931 DATA 2,4,5
932 DATA DARKNESS
933 DATA 1,1,9
934 DATA IRREGULAR HEARTBEATS
935 DATA 1,2,0
936 DATA LIGHTNING
937 DATA 1,9,0
938 DATA DOCTORS
939 DATA 1,2,7
940 DATA PEOPLE WITH DEFORMITIES
941 DATA 1,6,7
942 DATA MAKING MISTAKES
943 DATA 1,6,0
944 DATA LOOKING FOOLISH
```

```
945 DATA 1,5,Ø
946 DATA LOSING CONTROL
947 DATA 1,6,7
948 DATA FAINTING
949 DATA 3,1,Ø
95Ø DATA BECOMING NAUSEOUS
951 DATA 1,2,Ø
952 DATA SPIDERS
953 DATA 1,8,Ø
954 DATA TAKING RESPONSIBILITY
955 DATA 1,6,Ø
956 DATA KNIVES OR OTHER SHARP OBJECTS
957 DATA 1,2,1Ø
958 DATA THE IDEA OF GOING CRAZY
959 DATA 1,2,3
96Ø DATA DEALING WITH THE OPPOSITE SEX
961 DATA 1,5,6
962 DATA A SUDDEN LULL IN CONVERSATION
963 DATA 1,6,Ø
964 DATA FEELING DIFFERENT FROM OTHERS
965 DATA 2,5,Ø
966 DATA BEING TOUCHED
967 DATA 1,7,Ø
968 DATA TAKING TESTS
969 DATA 1,6,Ø
97Ø REM----------------------CATEGORIES
971 DATA DEATH
972 DATA ILLNESS
973 DATA LOSS OF CONTROL
974 DATA ISOLATION
975 DATA REJECTION
976 DATA FAILURE
977 DATA AUTHORITY FIGURES
978 DATA LIVING THINGS
979 DATA ENVIRONMENTS
98Ø DATA INANIMATE OBJECTS
```

# PART 5
# GAMES AND GRAPHICS

# CHAPTER 12 CONVERSION ROUTINES

You *must* read this chapter before you try typing any of the five programs listed in this part of the book. Otherwise, they *will not work!*

## Conversion Routines

Take a look at the last part of "Hexed," the program listed in pages 129 through 131 in Chapter 13. Values must be inserted in a "conversion routine" on program lines 9000 through 9200 to adapt this program to the graphics system of your computer. You must add the same routine to the same lines of all the other programs in this part of the book: "Barricade," "Clock," "Adult Hangman," and "Hunt the Snake."

Precise details of the conversion routine are not included in the listing of each program, because the routine will depend on which computer you own. This chapter supplies the routines that apply to the most widely used computer brands. Find the one for your computer, type it, and save it on disk or tape. Then load it immediately before you begin typing any of the programs in this part of the book.

If I haven't provided a conversion routine for your particular computer, at the end of this chapter you'll find "Conversion Routines for Other Computers" to tell you how to devise a routine of your own.

*Note!* All the conversion routines have been designed to work with computers that have *not been modified* in any way. If you use a plug-in accessory such as an 80-column video display board, or upper- and lowercase adapter, it should be disabled or unplugged.

### *Conversion Routine for the IBM PC and PCjr*

```
9000 K0=0
9010 K1=80
9020 K2=25
9030 K3=2
9040 K4=160
9050 K5=219
9060 K6=32
9070 K7=0
9100 DEF SEG=&HB000
9200 RETURN
```

Include line 9100 if your IBM PC is *not* fitted with a graphics adapter board. If you own a PCjr, or if your IBM PC *does* display high-resolution graphics, or is hooked up to a color video monitor, you will need to type a different line 9100:

If you're not sure about this, type one of the programs including the first version of line 9100. Save the program, then run it. If it doesn't work, change line 9100 to the alternate form.

Note that the IBM PC displays 80 characters per line when you turn it on, but can display 40 characters per line instead. Some of the programs in this book look better in 40-character mode, especially the "Clock" program and the "Hexed" game. You can set it to 40 characters by adding one extra line to the conversion routine:

```
9110 WIDTH 40
```

You must also change two other lines to look like this (and PCjr owners should *always* substitute these two lines):

```
9010 K1=40
9040 K4=80
```

### *Conversion Routine for the Apple II*

```
9000 K0=80
9010 K1=40
9020 K2=24
9030 K3=1
9040 K4=40
9050 K5=32
9060 K6=160
9070 K7=-128
9080 K8=-16384
9090 K9=-16368
9100 PRINT"CONVERTING MEMORY";
9110 D=1024:DIM VM%(1120)
9120 FOR A=80 TO 360 STEP 40
9130 FOR B=A TO A+640 STEP 320
9140 FOR C=B TO B+39
9150 VM%(C)=D:D=D+1
9160 NEXT C
9170 PRINT".";
9180 NEXT B:D=D+8
9190 NEXT A
9200 HOME:RETURN
```

The conversion routine for the Apple II is longer than the routines for other computers because the

Apple II organizes its video memory in an unconventional way, which the routine has to "normalize." It takes more than 2K (two kilobytes) of memory to do this. If you have an early-model bare-minimum Apple II system, you may find that a few programs cause an OUT OF MEMORY error message because the conversion routine has sequestered too much memory for its purposes. The vast majority of Apple users should have no trouble, however.

Note that the Apple routine includes two extra constants, K8 and K9, that are not needed in the routines for other computers. These two extra constants will be used in game programs when scanning the Apple keyboard.

Because the Apple conversion routine takes about 15 seconds to execute, the PRINT statement on line 9170 is included to display a series of dots on the screen, signifying that the computer has not gone to sleep and is in fact busily working.

### *Conversion Routine for Commodore 64*

```
9000 K0=1024
9010 K1=40
9020 K2=25
9030 K3=1
9040 K4=40
9050 K5=160
9060 K6=32
9070 K7=64
9080 POKE 53281,0:POKE 53280,0
9090 PRINT CHR$(5);
9100 POKE 650,128
9200 RETURN
```

Since various plug-in Commodore accessories move video memory to different locations inside the computer, or alter the number of characters per video line, you should not use these gadgets when you type and run the programs in this book.

Lines 9080 and 9090 turn the screen black and the cursor white. Normally, you could choose these colors to suit yourself, but the games and graphics programs use POKE statements that may produce no visible results on some Commodore 64s unless the cursor is white and the screen is a color other than white.

Line 9100 makes all the keys on the keyboard repeat, which is useful in video games.

If you see nothing on the screen when you run a program containing POKE statements, substitute this expression instead of CLS (it is only required on some vintages of Commodore 64):

**POKE 53281,1: PRINT CHR$(147);: POKE 53281,0**

This will make POKEd characters visible.

### *Conversion Routine for the VIC-20*

```
9000 K0=256*PEEK(648)
9010 K1=22
9020 K2=23
9030 K3=1
9040 K4=22
9050 K5=160
9060 K6=32
9070 K7=64
9080 POKE 36879,8:PRINT CHR$(5);
9100 POKE 650,128
9200 RETURN
```

Line 9080 selects a black screen and white cursor, which may be necessary for POKEd graphics to be visible. Line 9100 makes all the keys repeat, which is useful in video games.

The VIC-20 displays only 22 characters per line,

which will restrict some of the games in this part of the book. You can try using one of the various video adapters that convert the VIC-2Ø to 4Ø or 8Ø characters per line. Unlike the other conversion routines, the VIC-2Ø routine is designed to be compatible with many such adapters, although I have not tested them all. Type and save your program *first,* then turn off the computer, plug in the adapter, activate it, load the program, and run it.

If your adapted video display consists of 4Ø characters per video line, type **K1=4Ø** on line 9Ø1Ø of the conversion routine, and **K4=4Ø** on line 9Ø4Ø. If your adapted video display shows 8Ø characters per line, type **K1=8Ø** and **K4=8Ø.**

### *Conversion Routine for TRS-8Ø Model II, III, or 4*

```
9ØØØ KØ=1536Ø
9Ø1Ø K1=64
9Ø2Ø K2=16
9Ø3Ø K3=1
9Ø4Ø K4=64
9Ø5Ø K5=191
9Ø6Ø K6=32
9Ø7Ø K7=Ø
92ØØ RETURN
```

If you use the Model 4 be sure that it is running in "Model III mode." Check your instruction manual if you are confused about this.

### *Conversion Routine for Osborne 1*

```
9000 K0=61440
9010 K1=52
9020 K2=24
9030 K3=1
9040 K4=128
9050 K5=150
9060 K6=32
9070 K7=0
9200 RETURN
```

## Conversion Routine for Other Computers

If your computer is not listed in the preceding section, you will need to look up some figures in your instruction manual—or consult your dealer or a local user group—to fill in the blank conversion routine at the end of this section. Please don't write to me asking for advice; this chapter contains all the facts and figures that I know.

On line 9000, **K0** = the starting address of video memory. If your manual includes a system memory map or video memory map, it should tell you the address of the top-left point on the video screen. The number may be shown in two forms: decimal and hexadecimal. The decimal number will seem to be "larger"; the hexadecimal number will be 4 characters long and may contain letters as well as numerals. The decimal number is the one you want. If in doubt, check with your dealer or a local user group for your brand of computer.

On line 9010, **K1** = the number of letters per line that your computer displays on its video screen.

On line 9020, **K2** = the number of lines of text that your computer displays on its video screen.

On line 9Ø3Ø, **K3** = the number that you must add to each video memory address to move rightward to the adjacent video memory address. On almost all computers, this number is 1, so write a 1 here if you're not sure.

On line 9Ø4Ø, **K4** = the number that must be added to each video memory address to move to the address immediately below it on the screen. If in doubt, write the same number you wrote for **K1** on line 9Ø1Ø.

Each letter or graphics symbol that your computer displays is identified by a code number, often called its ASCII code. Your manual should contain a list of these codes. On line 9Ø5Ø, **K5** = the code number that identifies the graphics symbol that is a solid square.

On line 9Ø6Ø, **K6** = the code number that identifies the symbol that is a blank space. This number is almost always 32.

Some computers use another code, different from the ASCII code, in POKE statements. To determine this code, take the number you assigned to **KØ** on line 9ØØØ of your conversion routine and add **4ØØ** to it. I'll call the result **N.**

Clear the screen, type **POKE N,65** (instead of **N,** type the number you just calculated as **KØ+4ØØ**), and press Enter. You should see a letter A appear somewhere on the screen. If you do, on line 9Ø7Ø of your conversion routine type **K7=Ø.**

If you see any letter or symbol other than a capital A, you will have to do some detective work to find the POKE code that *does* generate an A on the screen. Doing this by trial and error is laborious, so you can write a little program to do it for you:

```
1Ø N= (type the number you get from KØ+4ØØ)
2Ø FOR A=Ø TO 255
```

```
30 PRINT"POKE CODE";A
40 POKE N,A
50 A$=INKEY$
60 IF A$="" THEN 50
70 NEXT A
```

This little program is not, of course, part of your conversion routine. It is needed only to find the number that must be used in the POKE statement to produce a letter A on your video screen.

If you have an Apple II or Commodore computer, type **GET A$** instead of **A$=INKEY$** on line 50 of this little program.

Run the program. Press any key to make it advance from one character to the next. Every possible letter, number, and symbol will be displayed together with the test number that produces it. When a letter A is produced, interrupt the program, and make a note of the POKE code. *Subtract this number from 65* and use the result as the value of **K7** on line 9070 of your conversion routine. This result may be a negative number on some computers.

When you've figured out the numbers you need, you can write them all into the blank conversion routine to make it your own. Be careful to get the numbers right; otherwise, the programs that use this routine won't work properly.

```
9000 K0=
9010 K1=
9020 K2=
9030 K3=
9040 K4=
9050 K5=
9060 K6=
9070 K7=
9200 RETURN
```

## Technical Notes

You can skip the rest of this chapter if technical matters don't interest you.

The conversion routine for each computer enables generalized PEEK and POKE statements to control video graphics. These statements are slower and cruder than advanced graphics statements available on many modern computers. PEEK and POKE work on *any* memory-mapped video system, whereas graphics statements such as PLOT or DRAW are usually not portable.

The only special case is the Apple II, whose low-resolution memory map is not made up of sequential, contiguous addresses. The addresses must first be reordered and assigned to **VM%(8Ø)** through **VM%(1Ø39)**—an array that *is* sequential and contiguous. The extra section of the Apple conversion routine takes care of this. PEEK and POKE statements must then refer to the array, not directly to the memory addresses. Because the array is specified as consisting of integers, it consumes only about 23ØØ bytes. It is dimensioned below and above the "video range" **VM%(8Ø)** through **VM%(1Ø39)** because some PEEK statements in a couple of the game programs will "look at" locations a little outside of video memory; error messages will ensue if the array does not include those "extra" addresses.

# CHAPTER 13
# HEXED

In most video games, quick reflexes count for more than quiet thought. "Hexed," however, is different. It's a test of pure logic, and you can take as long as you like to figure out how to win.

The program displays 19 letters of the alphabet in a hexagonal pattern (hence the game's title). When you type one of the letters on the keyboard, a square lights beside it on the screen. The object of the game is to light squares beside all the letters—which would be easy enough, except for one little snag. Each time you light one square, you reverse the state of all the squares around it. The ones with squares already lighted are turned off, and vice versa, so that turning on one part of the pattern tends to have the inconvenient effect of turning off other parts.

## How to Use It

You have the option of beginning with none of the "Hexed" squares lighted, or with a few of them lighted at random. This second option challenges you with a different pattern each time, and then allows you to choose an easy, medium, or hard game by typing a number from 1 through 9.

When the computer displays your starting pattern, type a few letters and watch the results. If you make a move that you don't like, type that letter again, and the pattern will reverse itself, back to the way it was before.

There's no limit to the number of moves you make, but if you get bored and want to end the game, type Z.

If you win the game by lighting all the squares on the screen, the program tells you how your score compared with the "par score"—the usual minimum number of moves necessary to win, beginning with that particular starting pattern.

## Adapting It for Your Computer

Before you start typing this program, you must read Chapter 12, find the conversion routine for your computer, and insert it on lines 9000 through 9200. Otherwise, the program will not work.

The screen-clearing command **CLS** appears on lines 20, 200, 300, and 900. The statement **A$=INKEY$** appears on lines 160, 240, 700, and 970. Check Chapter 2 if your computer doesn't understand these words.

If you have a TRS-80, type **RND(0)** instead of **RND(1)** in the middle of the expression on line 610.

Apple II users must retype line 440 so that it looks like this:

```
440 HX(B)=VM%(N)
```

## How It Works

Since the logic of this game is quite complicated, a line-by-line explanation would take up a lot of space. Instead, I'll provide a few general notes.

The program begins with instructions for using it, and then asks the player to choose a blank game board or one with some squares already lighted. This choice of game, 1 or 2, is recorded in variable **G.**

If **G=2,** the program asks the player how difficult a game is wanted. The number the player types (1 through 9) is doubled; 2 is added to it; the total is assigned to variable **C,** as the number of cycles the program will go through in creating a random starting pattern on the screen. When the program does this, it starts with all the letters lighted, then turns some out at random, **C** times. You can see this happening when you begin playing the game. If you were able to memorize these random computer moves and enter them yourself in reverse order, you would return to the starting position with all squares lighted. In practice, for any level of difficulty greater than 1, the computer makes too many moves, too fast, for them to be memorized.

The most complicated part of the program is on lines 3ØØ through 45Ø, where the video memory location of each letter in the pattern is recorded in **HX(1)** through **HX(4Ø).** This would be a simple routine if it applied to just one computer, but I had to generalize it for all computers.

**VL(1)** through **VL(4Ø)** are used to store the "value" of each position in the pattern. Each turned-on letter has value 2; each turned-off letter has value 1; "extra" positions around the edges of the pattern have value Ø. These extra positions are not used, but must exist to satisfy the logic later in the program.

Each time a pattern location changes from off to on, the appropriate **VL( )** number is increased from 1 to 2 and vice versa. Variable **T** is used as a running total of all the **VL** numbers (see line 83Ø). If **T=38,** all the 19 letter locations have been switched on, so the player has won the game (see line 74Ø).

If the player has selected game version 2, lines 6ØØ through 62Ø install the preliminary random pattern on the screen.

Lines 7ØØ through 75Ø look for keyboard input.

Since this game can be difficult to finish, I've allowed the player to give up at any time by typing a Z. Otherwise, the player types any letter from A through S to change the status of a letter on the screen. The ASCII code of this input is converted into a number that corresponds to the way the video display is numbered and is stored in variable **P.**

Variable **TL** is the total number of moves the player has made so far.

The subroutine on lines 8ØØ through 85Ø flips the square beside the chosen letter on the screen from off to on (or on to off), then examines each adjacent letter, changes its state, and changes the value **VL(Q)** accordingly. Last, line 84Ø updates the actual video image.

## Going Further

This game is difficult to modify significantly. If you really want to alter it, you should go back to first principles. Buy or make a set of counters, black on one side and white on the other, such as are used in the game Othello. Experiment arranging them in different patterns. I used a hexagon array; would a square work as well? Or a triangle? Play the game by flipping the counters over instead of lighting squares on the video screen. If you find a variation that you think works well, study the logic involved, and figure out how it could be converted into a computer program of your own.

This is exactly what I did when I devised "Hexed." Your program should be easier to write than mine, because you can design it specifically for your computer. You can use PRINT AT or LOCATE statements that are specific to your version of BASIC, to position and light squares on the screen via PRINT statements instead of by POKEing video memory. This should be a lot easier, especially if you arrange your letters in a square layout. Try it, and you may end up with an improved game that's all your own.

```
10 REM                              HEXED
20 CLS
30 GOSUB 9000
40 PRINT"IN THIS GAME, YOU HAVE TO"
50 PRINT"LIGHT UP A SQUARE BESIDE"
60 PRINT"EVERY LETTER IN A PATTERN ON"
70 PRINT"THE SCREEN, BY TYPING THE"
80 PRINT"LETTERS ON THE KEYBOARD."
90 PRINT
100 PRINT"BUT EACH LETTER YOU TYPE"
110 PRINT"REVERSES THE STATE OF THE"
120 PRINT"SQUARES AROUND IT.":PRINT
130 PRINT"DO YOU WANT TO...":PRINT
140 PRINT"1:BEGIN WITH NO LETTERS LIT?"
150 PRINT"2:BEGIN WITH RANDOM PATTERN?"
160 A$=INKEY$
170 R=RND(1)
180 IF A$<"1" OR A$>"2" THEN 160
190 G=VAL(A$):IF G=1 THEN 300
197 REM
198 REM-----------------HARD/EASY GAME
199 REM
200 CLS
210 PRINT"TYPE A NUMBER FROM 1 TO 9"
220 PRINT"TO SELECT GAME DIFFICULTY."
230 PRINT:PRINT"(1=EASY ... 9=HARD)"
240 A$=INKEY$
250 IF A$<"1" OR A$>"9" THEN 240
260 C=2*VAL(A$)+2
297 REM
298 REM------------------SET VARIABLES
299 REM
300 CLS
320 DIM HX(40),VL(40),AZ(19)
330 TL=0:T=19*G:K8=K5+K6:H=8:V=3
340 IF K1=80 THEN 400
350 IF K1>40 THEN H=6:GOTO 400
```

```
360 IF K1=40 THEN H=4:GOTO 400
370 H=4:V=5
400 X=K0+K3+(2*K4)+(H*K3)
410 A=(V*K4)-K3*(H/2):B=10
420 FOR M=X TO X+(4*A) STEP A
430 FOR N=M TO M+(4*H*K3) STEP H*K3
440 HX(B)=N
450 B=B+1:NEXT N:NEXT M
497 REM
498 REM-----------------VIDEO GAME BOARD
499 REM
500 PRINT"TYPE LETTERS A-S.     Z=END."
510 FOR N=1 TO 7:READ M:NEXT N
520 FOR N=1 TO 19:READ M:AZ(N)=M
530 POKE HX(M)-K3,N+64-K7:VL(M)=1
540 IF G=2 THEN POKE HX(M),K5:VL(M)=2
550 NEXT N:IF G=1 THEN 700
570 DATA 0,-6,-5,1,6,5,-1
580 DATA 10,11,12,15,16,17,18,20,21,22
590 DATA 23,24,26,27,28,29,32,33,34
597 REM
598 REM--------------FILL IN RND DISPLAY
599 REM
600 FOR M=1 TO C
610 P=AZ(INT(RND(1)*19)+1)
620 GOSUB 800:NEXT M
697 REM
698 REM-------------------KEYBOARD ENTRY
699 REM
700 A$=INKEY$
710 IF A$="Z" THEN 900
720 IF A$<"A" OR A$>"S" THEN 700
730 P=AZ(ASC(A$)-64):TL=TL+1:GOSUB 800
740 IF T=38 THEN 900
750 GOTO 700
797 REM
798 REM-------------------UPDATE DISPLAY
799 REM
800 RESTORE
810 FOR N=1 TO 7:READ Q:Q=Q+P
820 IF VL(Q)=0 THEN 850
830 VL(Q)=3-VL(Q):T=T+(2*VL(Q))-3
```

```
840 A=PEEK(HX(Q)):POKE HX(Q),K8-A
850 NEXT N:RETURN
897 REM
898 REM---------------------END OF GAME
899 REM
900 CLS
910 IF T<38 THEN 960
920 PRINT"CONGRATULATIONS! YOU WIN."
930 PRINT:IF G=1 THEN 960
940 PRINT"YOU MADE";TL;"MOVES."
950 PRINT"PAR SCORE WAS";C;"."
960 PRINT:PRINT"PLAY AGAIN?"
970 A$=INKEY$
980 IF A$="Y" THEN RUN
985 IF A$="N" THEN END
990 GOTO 970
8997 REM
8998 REM-------------CONVERSION ROUTINE
8999 REM
9000 K0=
9010 K1=
9020 K2=
9030 K3=
9040 K4=
9050 K5=
9060 K6=
9070 K7=

     (If your
     conversion
     routine
     requires
     extra lines,
     add them here.
     See Chapter 12.)

9200 RETURN
```

# CHAPTER 14
# BARRICADE

Most video games written in BASIC simply don't run fast enough. The graphics jump around in jerky steps, instead of gliding and zooming smoothly as they do in arcade games. Also, it's hard to write BASIC games that entail any real strategy.

The program in this chapter tries to rise above both these limitations. It's not a new concept—a two-player version was in the arcades several years ago, and a more recent version appeared as a tie-in with a Walt Disney movie. I think I've improved the computer strategy, however, so that the version here is more challenging.

The idea is simple enough. The computer draws a line across the screen. The line keeps growing and attempts to encircle another line that you are drawing at the same time. If you become boxed in, or if you make an error and your line crashes into the screen border or any other line on the screen, you lose. If you trap the computer's line and force it to crash, you win.

## How to Use It

When you run the program, it tells you how to move your screen marker left, right, up, and down with keys 1, 2, A, and Z.

To start the game, type one initial of your name.

The screen clears, the computer's marker starts drawing a line of asterisks, and your marker starts drawing a line made up of your initial. There is no way to stop; to avoid crashing into the border or the computer's trail of asterisks, you must change the direction in which your line is growing by pressing key 1, 2, A, or Z. Whoever crashes first loses. The program flashes the crashed marker a few times to show where the collision occurred.

## Adapting It for Your Computer

You *must* add the appropriate conversion routine on lines 9000 through 9200 before you try to run this program (see Chapter 12). Without this routine, the program won't work at all.

The expression **A$=INKEY$** appears on lines 105, 700, and 1210, and the word **CLS** appears on lines 600, 1000, and 2000. Check Chapter 2 if your computer doesn't understand either of these words.

If you have an Apple II, you must retype line 110 to look like this:

```
PP=PEEK(K8):IF PP>K6 THEN A$=CHR$(PP+K7)
```

If you have a TRS-80, type **RND(0)** instead of **RND(1)** in the expressions on lines 230 and 2010.

For the game to work on the Apple II, you must rewrite every PEEK and POKE statement. Lines 50, 160, 170, 200, 210, 220, 240, 250, 260, 270, 280, 290, 560, 570, 2120, 2140, and 2200 are affected. Apple II users must change them all, as follows.

Take the single letter you find after each POKE word, enclose it in parentheses, and insert **VM%** between POKE and the parentheses. For example, instead of **POKE X,P** type **POKE VM%(X),P** on line 17Ø.

Wherever you find the word PEEK, make a similar change, remembering to add parentheses before *and after* the statement. For example, instead of **PEEK(Y+DY)** type **PEEK(VM%(Y+DY))** on line 2ØØ. Instead of **PEEK(Y+T*2)** type **PEEK(VM%(Y+T*2))** on line 25Ø. And so on. Remember, these changes are required only for the Apple II. Make them carefully, and save your program before you run it.

Where the expression **C=42** appears on line 2Ø6Ø, Apple users should type **C=42–K7** instead. Other computer users may need to do this if the computer displays a line consisting of some character other than asterisks when running the game.

## How It Works

As has already been mentioned in the "Phone Words" program (see pages 89–9Ø), the computer takes longer to obey GOTO statements involving high line numbers. **GOTO 5ØØØØ,** for instance, is executed more slowly than **GOTO 5Ø.** Consequently, to make this game as fast as possible, its most active parts have been put at the beginning of the program where line numbers are lowest. Lines 5Ø through 37Ø control the actual playing of the game; the instructions and screen layout appear as a subroutine on lines 1ØØØ through 221Ø.

Line by line, it works like this:

3Ø–4Ø

**GOSUB 9ØØØ** refers to the conversion routine, which must be executed before anything else. **GOSUB 1ØØØ** displays instructions and prepares the screen layout. The action then jumps to the player's move starting on line 100.

100–140

**DX,** the direction of the player's marker, is copied temporarily into **A.** The keyboard is scanned to see if the player wants to alter this value.

150

Provided the new value of **A** isn't the opposite of the old direction, **DX,** value **A** is assigned to **DX;** that is, the player is not allowed to double back.

160

The player's location, **X,** is changed by **DX.** If the new position is not a blank area of the screen, the player has crashed, and the action ends on line 400.

170–190

The player's initial is POKEd into the video display. If the number of moves so far, **N,** is less than a randomly selected minimum, **R,** the computer's direction, **DY,** is made opposite to **DX.**

200–370

The computer's move is complex, especially because the logic has been compressed as much as possible. Its strategy is to look ahead 1, 2, and 3 squares (lines 200, 210, 220) and record, in **U,** how many squares ahead are unobstructed. If an obstruction lies ahead, the program randomly decides whether to look left or right on line 230. It then looks ahead 1, 2, and 3 squares in that direction and stores the number of clear squares in **V** (lines 240–260). If that way is obstructed, it looks in the opposite direction. Depending on the values of **U** and **V,** it chooses the best compromise, depending on which direction is least obstructed. For instance, if there is an obstruction 3 squares ahead, but no obstruction to the left, it turns left. Note that the computer is not aware at any time of the player's location; its tactics are evasive instead of aggressive. This quality is not always apparent when the game is in progress.

4ØØ–58Ø

The program flashes the marker that has just crashed. The **N** loops are delay loops, to adjust the rate of flashing.

12ØØ–124Ø

At the beginning of the game, the player is asked to type an initial. While the computer waits, it repeatedly gets new **RND(1)** values to advance the random-number generator to a new arbitrary value, so that the computer won't always make the same move when the program is first loaded and run.

2Ø1Ø–221Ø

Random value **R** is the preliminary number of moves during which the computer's marker will move in the exact opposite direction of the player's marker to avoid capture in the early part of the game. The starting positions **X** and **Y** of the player and computer are established, with their initial directions **DX** and **DY. D,** on line 2Ø5Ø, is a delay factor to control the speed of the game. **C,** on line 2Ø6Ø, is the code of the computer's marker. A border is drawn around the edge of the screen to limit the play area, and the setup routine RETURNs.

## Going Further

If you don't want the computer's marker to be an asterisk, type some ASCII code other than 42 on line 2Ø6Ø.

If the game is too fast, on line 2Ø5Ø type **D=3Ø** or **D=4Ø** instead of **D=2Ø** to increase the delay factor. To quicken the game, type **D=1Ø** or **D=1.**

If you don't like using keys 1, 2, A, and Z to control your marker on the screen, change lines 11Ø through 14Ø so that other characters appear within the quote marks to move the marker up, down, left, and right, respectively. Then change the instructions on lines 1110 through 1140 to match.

If you have joysticks, you can adapt lines 110 through 140 to make the computer look for joystick codes. Check your manual for the joystick codes used by your computer.

You could alter the game so that two people play against each other. Instead of the computer's move, substitute a second player's move in the section made up of lines 100 through 170. Naturally, the second player will have to use a different set of keys to control the direction of a marker on the screen. Variable **Y** will be used to represent the player's position, instead of the computer's. The same setup routine from line 1000 onward can be retained, although it will need to ask the second player for an initial.

You can also rewrite the program so that it keeps score. Use two variables, such as **CS** and **PS,** to store the computer's score and the player's score. One snag: if the player asks for another game, line 710 uses the word **RUN** to restart the program from scratch. But RUN resets everything (including any scores!) to zero. So, instead of **RUN** type **GOTO 40** on line 710.

If you make this alteration and play the game many times, obsolete values of **A$** will pile up in computer memory each time the **A$=INKEY$** statement is executed on line 100. When memory is full, "garbage collection" occurs as the old values of **A$** are thrown out. The program pauses while this happens. On some modern systems, the pause lasts less than a second.

```
10 REM                              BARRICADE
20 REM
30 GOSUB 9000
40 GOSUB 1000:GOTO 100
50 Y=Y+DY:POKE Y,C
60 FOR B=1 TO D:NEXT
97 REM
98 REM--------------------PLAYER'S MOVE
99 REM
100 A=DX
105 A$=INKEY$
110 IF A$="A" THEN A=-K4
120 IF A$="Z" THEN A=K4
130 IF A$="1" THEN A=-K3
140 IF A$="2" THEN A=K3
150 IF DX+A<>0 THEN DX=A
160 X=X+DX:IF PEEK(X)<>K6 THEN 400
170 POKE X,P
190 IF N<R THEN N=N+1:DY=-DX
197 REM
198 REM----------------COMPUTER'S MOVE
199 REM
200 U=0:IF PEEK(Y+DY)<>K6 THEN 230
210 U=1:IF PEEK(Y+DY*2)=K6 THEN U=2
220 IF PEEK(Y+DY*3)=K6 AND U=2 THEN 50
230 N=K1:T=SGN(RND(1)-.5)*(K8-ABS(DY))
240 V=0:IF PEEK(Y+T)<>K6 THEN 270
250 V=1:IF PEEK(Y+T*2)=K6 THEN V=2
260 IF PEEK(Y+3*T)=K6 AND V=2 THEN 350
270 IF PEEK(Y-T)<>K6 THEN 300
280 V=V+3:IF PEEK(Y-T*2)=K6 THEN V=6
290 IF PEEK(Y-T*3)=K6 AND V=6 THEN 370
300 IF U=2 THEN 50
310 ON V GOTO 340,350,360,340,350,370
320 IF U=1 THEN 50
330 GOTO 500
340 IF U=1 THEN 50
350 DY=T:GOTO 50
360 IF U=1 THEN 50
370 DY=-T:GOTO 50
397 REM
398 REM---------------------END OF GAME
```

```
399 REM
400 A=X:B=P:GOTO 550
500 A=Y:B=C
550 FOR M=1 TO 5
560 POKE A,K6:FOR N=1 TO 200:NEXT N
570 POKE A,B:FOR N=1 TO 200:NEXT N
580 NEXT M
600 CLS
610 IF B=C THEN PRINT"YOU";
620 IF B=P THEN PRINT"THE COMPUTER";
630 PRINT" WON.":PRINT
640 PRINT"PLAY AGAIN?"
700 A$=INKEY$
710 IF A$="Y" THEN 40
720 IF A$="N" THEN END
730 GOTO 700
997 REM
998 REM-------------------START OF GAME
999 REM
1000 CLS
1010 PRINT"IN THIS GAME, YOU AND THE"
1020 PRINT"COMPUTER TRY TO DRAW LINES"
1030 PRINT"AROUND EACH OTHER. WHOEVER"
1040 PRINT"GETS TRAPPED FIRST, LOSES."
1050 PRINT:PRINT
1100 PRINT"TO DRAW YOUR LINE, USE:"
1105 PRINT
1110 PRINT"1 TO MOVE LEFT"
1120 PRINT"2 TO MOVE RIGHT"
1130 PRINT"A TO MOVE UP"
1140 PRINT"Z TO MOVE DOWN"
1150 PRINT
1200 PRINT"TYPE YOUR INITIAL TO BEGIN:"
1210 A$=INKEY$
1220 IF A$="" THEN R=RND(1):GOTO 1210
1230 IF A$<"A" OR A$>"Z" THEN 1210
1240 P=ASC(A$)-K7
1997 REM
1998 REM-----------------PREPARE SCREEN
1999 REM
2000 CLS
2010 R=INT(RND(1)*K1/2)+K1/2
```

```
2020 X=K0+K4*INT(.35*K2)+K3*INT(.35*K1)
2030 Y=K0+K4*INT(.65*K2)+K3*INT(.65*K1)
2040 DX=K3:DY=-K3:K8=K4+K3
2050 D=20
2060 C=42
2100 A=K4*(K2-1):B=K3*(K1-1)
2110 FOR N=K0 TO K0+B STEP K3
2120 POKE N,K5:POKE N+A,K5:NEXT
2130 FOR N=K0 TO K0+A STEP K4
2140 POKE N,K5:POKE N+B,K5:NEXT
2200 POKE X,P:POKE Y,C:N=0
2210 RETURN
8997 REM
8998 REM-------------CONVERSION ROUTINE
8999 REM
9000 K0=
9010 K1=
9020 K2=
9030 K3=
9040 K4=
9050 K5=
9060 K6=
9070 K7=

     (If your
     conversion
     routine
     requires
     extra lines,
     add them here.
     See Chapter 12.)

9200 RETURN
```

# CHAPTER 15
# CLOCK

If you're like most people, you can't always use your computer as much as you'd wish. All too often, you have to turn away from the friendly glow of its video screen to deal with tiresome, humdrum tasks such as eating, sleeping, and conversing with family and friends. During these periods, your computer sits lifeless and forlorn, with empty memory and idle microprocessor.

Well, here's a program that gives your system something useful to do when you're not using it to do anything else. It turns your computer into a not-very-accurate, marginally functional digital clock.

## How to Use It

When you run the program, it takes a few moments to READ its DATA, which it will use to create large numerals on the screen. Then it asks you to type the current time in hours, minutes, and seconds, as a series of 6 digits. If it's earlier than 1Ø o'clock, you must precede the "hours" numeral with a Ø. Likewise, precede the "minutes" numeral with a Ø if the time is less than 1Ø minutes past the hour. Don't put any punctuation between the numerals. When you type the seconds, use a value about 3Ø seconds later than the current time.

If you type in an illegal time, greater than 125959

or less than **ØlØØØØ**, the program rejects it and makes you start again from the beginning. Assuming you have typed an acceptable time, the program waits for you to press any key to start the clock. Do this when the real time is just 2 seconds earlier than the time you typed.

The program now displays hours, minutes, and seconds in large numerals at the top of the screen. On an 8-inch monitor, the numerals are about 1 inch high—easily visible from across the room.

Compare the seconds display with the seconds shown by a real digital watch or clock, and adjust the speed of the program by typing F to make it run faster or S to make it run slower. You must hit the key several times to produce a noticeable effect.

When you have the speed just right, interrupt the program, type **PRINT FS,** and press the Enter key. Make a note of the number that is displayed. List the program and type that number on line 60 as the new initial value for the **FS** variable. In my listing, I have **FS=24Ø,** but your computer may need a different value. After you have made this alteration, save the program to make a permanent record, so you won't need to calibrate your clock next time you run it.

The program displays the caption **$1ØØØ DIGITAL CLOCK** while it is running. If your system cost more or less than $1ØØØ, you may want to change the PRINT statement on line 52Ø accordingly.

## Adapting It for Your Computer

Before you try to run this program, you *must* add a conversion routine on lines 9ØØØ through 92ØØ. See Chapter 12 for the routine appropriate to your computer.

The word **CLS** appears on lines 2Ø, 2ØØ, and 5ØØ, and the expression **A$=INKEY$** occurs on lines

300, 440, and 610. If your computer doesn't understand either of these statements, see Chapter 2.

If you own an Apple II, you can replace the **A$=INKEY$** statements with **GET A$,** except on line 610, which must look like this:

```
610 PP=PEEK(K9):POKE K8,0:A$="":IF PP>K6
    THEN A$=CHR$(PP+K7)
```

Apple II users will need to make two more modifications. Type lines 570 and 740 like this:

```
570 POKE VM%(X(A)+(6*K3)+(B*K4)),K5

740 POKE VM%(C),T%(CK(M),A):A=A+1
```

## How It Works

You'd think that making a computer count hours, minutes, and seconds would be a simple operation. The large digital display entails some complications, however. Line by line, it works like this:

30–40
: First the program refers to the conversion routine; then it READs through DATA on line 695 to get to the graphics DATA on lines 800–815, which determine the appearance of the large display numerals that will be used.

50–60
: The **T%( )** array will store the graphics DATA to generate the display numerals; **CK(0)** through **CK(5)** will store the time value of each clock digit; **X(0)** through **X(5)** will store the starting video address of each display numeral. **FS** is the fast/slow adjustment value.

70–180
: Addresses are calculated for **X( )**. Graphics DATA are stored in **T%( )**.

290–340
The user types the current time. Each digit is assigned to **CK( ).** To simplify this process and enable error trapping, a loop scans the keyboard 6 times for individually typed digits.

550–590
These loops display 2 colons on the screen to separate the pairs of clock digits. It's an elaborate process because it must work with any video display. **GOSUB 700** displays the clock digits themselves.

610–630
The program checks to see whether the user is typing F or S. If so, the program cycles back to see if any further keystrokes are forthcoming.

640–695
This counting routine advances the seconds, minutes, and hours. DATA on line 695 give the maximum value for each clock digit; thus if the first digit (counting seconds) reaches 10, it resets to 0, and the next digit (counting 10s of seconds) increases by 1. The routine is complicated because we count time in 60s (seconds, minutes) and 12s (hours).

700–750
The shape of a new digit is POKEd into video memory. If only the rightmost digit needs to be updated, the computer has to execute the delay loop from 1 to **FS.** If more than one digit needs to be updated, the display process takes sufficiently long that the delay loop can be skipped.

## Going Further

The clock looks best on a video display of 40 characters per line. If your computer offers you an option of 40 or 80 characters, you may want to add a line to the program to force it into 40-character mode. Change your conversion routine accordingly, by halving the values assigned to **K1** and **K4** normally used for your 8Ø-column display.

The DATA statements on lines 8ØØ through 815 have been devised so that you can see the shape of the display numerals that these statements will create. Each 1 indicates a solid square; each Ø is a blank. You can create your own numerals by substituting your own pattern of 1s and Øs in these lines of DATA.

```
10 REM                                    CLOCK
20 CLS
30 GOSUB 9000
40 FOR A=1 TO 7:READ B:NEXT A
47 REM
48 REM---------------ESTABLISH CONSTANTS
49 REM
50 DIM T%(9,24),CK(5),X(5)
60 FS=240
70 FOR A=0 TO 5
80 X(A)=K0+K4+K3*(1+(A*5)+4*INT(A/2))
90 NEXT A
100 PRINT"READING DATA";
110 FOR A=0 TO 5 STEP 5
120 FOR B=0 TO 20 STEP 4:PRINT".";
130 FOR C=A TO A+4
140 READ N$
150 FOR D=1 TO 4:A$=MID$(N$,D,1)
160 E=K6:IF A$="1" THEN E=K5
170 T%(C,D+B)=E
180 NEXT D:NEXT C:NEXT B:NEXT A
197 REM
198 REM---------------------INSTRUCTIONS
199 REM
200 CLS
210 PRINT"TYPE THE EXACT TIME IN"
220 PRINT"HOURS, MINUTES, AND SECONDS"
230 PRINT"USING SIX DIGITS WITH"
240 PRINT"NO SPACES BETWEEN THEM."
```

```
250 PRINT
260 PRINT"E.G. FOR 2:07 AND 5 SECONDS"
270 PRINT"YOU WOULD TYPE 020705.":PRINT
280 PRINT"TIME: ";
290 B=0:C=100000:FOR A=0 TO 5
300 A$=INKEY$
310 IF A$<"0" OR A$>"9" THEN 300
320 PRINT A$;:CK(A)=VAL(A$)
330 B=B+(C*CK(A)):C=INT(C/10)
340 NEXT A
350 IF B>125959 OR B<10000 THEN 200
400 PRINT:PRINT
410 PRINT"TO ADJUST SPEED WHILE CLOCK"
420 PRINT"IS RUNNING, PRESS F OR S."
430 PRINT:PRINT"PRESS ANY KEY TO START"
440 A$=INKEY$
450 IF A$="" THEN 440
497 REM
498 REM--------------------SET UP DISPLAY
499 REM
500 CLS
510 FOR A=1 TO 10:PRINT:NEXT
520 PRINT TAB(10)"$1000 DIGITAL CLOCK"
530 PRINT
540 PRINT TAB(9)"(SLIGHTLY INACCURATE)"
550 FOR A=1 TO 3 STEP 2
560 FOR B=2 TO 5 STEP 3
570 POKE X(A)+(6*K3)+(B*K4),K5
580 NEXT B:NEXT A
590 N=0:GOSUB 700
597 REM
598 REM--------------COUNT HRS/MINS/SECS
599 REM
600 N=5:RESTORE
610 A$=INKEY$
620 IF A$="F" THEN FS=FS-1:GOTO 610
630 IF A$="S" THEN FS=FS+1:GOTO 610
640 READ L:CK(N)=CK(N)+1
650 IF CK(N)<L THEN GOSUB 700:GOTO 600
```

```
660 CK(N)=Ø:N=N-1:IF ABS(N)<>1 THEN 64Ø
67Ø IF N=-1 THEN N=Ø:CK(1)=1:GOTO 65Ø
68Ø IF CK(Ø)=1 THEN READ L
69Ø GOTO 64Ø
695 DATA 1Ø,6,1Ø,6,1Ø,3,2
697 REM
698 REM------------------UPDATE DISPLAY
699 REM
7ØØ IF N=5 THEN FOR D=1 TO FS:NEXT D
71Ø FOR M=5 TO N STEP -1:A=1
72Ø FOR B=X(M) TO X(M)+(5*K4) STEP K4
73Ø FOR C=B TO B+(3*K3) STEP K3
74Ø POKE C,T%(CK(M),A):A=A+1
75Ø NEXT C:NEXT B:NEXT M:RETURN
798 REM------------------------NUMERALS
799 REM
8ØØ DATA 1111,11ØØ,1111,1111,1ØØØ
8Ø1 DATA 1ØØ1,Ø1ØØ,ØØØ1,ØØØ1,1Ø1Ø
8Ø2 DATA 1ØØ1,Ø1ØØ,1111,Ø111,1Ø1Ø
8Ø3 DATA 1ØØ1,Ø1ØØ,1ØØØ,ØØØ1,1111
8Ø4 DATA 1ØØ1,Ø1ØØ,1ØØØ,ØØØ1,ØØ1Ø
8Ø5 DATA 1111,111Ø,1111,1111,ØØ1Ø
8Ø9 REM
81Ø DATA 1111,1111,1111,1111,1111
811 DATA 1ØØØ,1ØØØ,ØØØ1,1ØØ1,1ØØ1
812 DATA 1111,1111,ØØØ1,1111,1111
813 DATA ØØØ1,1ØØ1,ØØØ1,1ØØ1,ØØØ1
814 DATA ØØØ1,1ØØ1,ØØØ1,1ØØ1,ØØØ1
815 DATA 1111,1111,ØØØ1,1111,Ø111
8997 REM
8998 REM-------------CONVERSION ROUTINE
8999 REM
9ØØØ KØ=
9Ø1Ø K1=
9Ø2Ø K2=
9Ø3Ø K3=
9Ø4Ø K4=
9Ø5Ø K5=
9Ø6Ø K6=
```

```
9Ø7Ø K7=

     (If your
     conversion
     routine
     requires
     extra lines,
     add them here.
     See Chapter 12.)

92ØØ RETURN
```

# CHAPTER 16
# ADULT HANGMAN

The title of this chapter doesn't mean that the program is "X-rated." Nor is it an interactive adventure featuring the exploits of a middle-aged medieval executioner. It's simply a version of the Hangman word game that elevates it to a new, adult level of skill.

## How to Use It

When you run the program, it asks how long a word you want. The built-in vocabulary contains words ranging from 4 to 9 letters long; generally, 5-letter and 6-letter words are the hardest to guess, because longer words tend to include repeated letters or other distinctive letter groupings that act as clues.

After you make your choice, the computer displays a line of dashes representing the secret word. It waits for you to start guessing letters, displays each letter you try, shows where each correctly guessed letter appears in the secret word, and stops you from guessing a letter you have already tried.

If a letter appears 2 or more times in the secret word, you need only to guess that letter once to be shown all its occurrences.

Each time you make a wrong guess, the computer draws another segment of a gallows and hanged man. Make 1Ø errors, and it's all over.

When you type this program, try to insert the correct number of spaces in the various PRINT statements so the text will be displayed correctly on the screen. Type 1 space between the quote marks on line 14Ø; type 1 space before the closing quote marks on lines 8Ø, 2ØØ, 24Ø, 33Ø, and 43Ø; type 1 space before the word LEFT and 4 spaces after it on line 46Ø; type 4 spaces after the word LOSE on line 61Ø; type 17 spaces after RIGHT! on line 49Ø.

## Converting It for Your Computer

Before you run this program, you *must* type a conversion routine on lines **9ØØØ** onward. See Chapter 12 for the conversion routine that applies to your particular computer.

The word **CLS** appears on lines 2Ø and 19Ø. The expression **A$=INKEY$** occurs on lines 1ØØ, 25Ø, and 66Ø. If your computer doesn't understand one or both of these statements, check Chapter 2. Note that on line 25Ø it is essential to retain the variable **L$** instead of the usual **A$.**

If you have a TRS-8Ø, substitute the statement **RND(Ø)** for **RND(1)** in the expression on line 15Ø.

The statement **LOCATE 1,1** appears on line 470 to home the cursor without clearing the screen. Alternate forms of this statement are listed in Chapter 2, but some computers don't offer this feature at all, in which case you must omit line 47Ø entirely.

Without this statement, scrolling occurs when the computer executes a number of PRINT statements. This, in turn, will disrupt the graphics; so you should omit the entire graphics section of the program on lines 1998 through 29ØØ, and omit the statement **GOSUB 2ØØØ** on line 43Ø. You can also omit the conversion routine on lines 9ØØØ onward, since this is not required if graphics are not used.

If your computer displays fewer than 4Ø characters per line, there won't be room on your screen for both the text and the graphics, so you will also have to omit the graphics routines. Follow the instructions in the preceding paragraph. (But do not omit the LOCATE statement, or its equivalent, on line 47Ø.)

Apple II users must type slightly different versions of lines 2Ø7Ø, 211Ø, 221Ø, 232Ø, 24ØØ, 251Ø, 26ØØ, 27ØØ, 281Ø, and 29ØØ. On these lines, enclose the character(s) following the word POKE in parentheses, and insert **VM%** before the parentheses. For example, instead of **POKE B,K5** type **POKE VM%(B),K5** on line 2Ø7Ø; instead of **POKE B+K3,62** type **POKE VM%(B+K3),62** on line 29ØØ. Make these changes carefully; a single error can stop the program from working. Be sure to save your program before you run it.

## How It Works

Important variables in this program include:

**SW$:** Secret word
**DW$:** Displayed portions of the word
**GL$:** Cumulative guessed letters
**LW:** Length of word
**RG:** Number of right guesses
**WG:** Number of wrong guesses
**X:** Video address of the start of gallows graphics

Line by line, the program works like this:

3Ø–8Ø
The conversion routine is executed, the starting address for the graphics is assigned to **X,** and instructions are displayed.

1ØØ–14Ø
The computer waits for the user to type a number between 4 and 9. While waiting, the RND function is sampled repeatedly to advance it to a fresh value.

150–180

The program assigns to **R** a random number from 0 through 99. The computer reads through the word list **R** times. If it runs out of words, it restores the list and starts over. If the length of the last word it reads is not the length that the user specified, the computer reads further until it finds a word of the correct length.

200–270

The program displays the secret word so far, and letters tried so far. If the player has guessed all the letters correctly, the game is won. If the player has guessed 10 wrong letters, the game is lost. Otherwise, the program asks for a new guess.

300–340

The player's new guess is checked against all previously guessed letters. If a match is found, **M=1;** otherwise, **M=0.** At the end of the search, if **M=0,** the guess is valid, and execution skips to line 400.

400–430

The player's guess is checked against each letter in the secret word. Each correct match activates subroutine 900, advancing the value of **M** by 1 and inserting the guessed letter in **DW$.** At the end of the search, if **M=0,** the guess was wrong, and line 430 invokes subroutine 2000, which draws the next piece of the gallows and the hanged man.

## Going Further

Add more words to the vocabulary to make the game as varied as possible. Type your words in DATA statements on new lines from 1070 through 1980. Do not add any new lines after 1990; that *must* remain the last entry. Your words can range in length from 4 to 9 letters. Mix the word lengths as randomly as possible.

If your computer offers a good range of graphics

characters, you can improve the display of the gallows and hanged man. Insert your own codes in the POKE statements on lines 2000 through 2900.

```
10 REM                          ADULT HANGMAN
20 CLS
30 GOSUB 9000:X=K0+(K4*5)+(K3*30)
40 PRINT"IN THIS GAME, THE COMPUTER"
50 PRINT"THINKS OF A WORD, AND YOU"
60 PRINT"TRY TO GUESS IT.":PRINT
70 PRINT"HOW LONG A WORD DO YOU WANT?"
80 PRINT"(LIMIT: 4 TO 9 LETTERS) ";
97 REM
98 REM---------------SELECT SECRET WORD
99 REM
100 A$=INKEY$
110 R=RND(1)
120 IF A$<"4" OR A$>"9" THEN 100
130 PRINT A$:LW=VAL(A$):RG=0:WG=0
140 GL$=" ":DW$=LEFT$("---------",LW)
150 R=INT(RND(1)*100):N=1
160 READ SW$:IF SW$="X" THEN RESTORE
170 N=N+1:IF N<R THEN 160
180 IF LEN(SW$)<>LW THEN 160
190 CLS
198 REM------------------GUESS A LETTER
199 REM
200 PRINT"THE SECRET WORD: ";DW$:PRINT
210 PRINT"LETTERS YOU'VE TRIED:";GL$
220 IF RG=LW THEN 500
230 IF WG=10 THEN 600
240 PRINT:PRINT"YOUR GUESS IS? ";
250 L$=INKEY$
260 IF L$<"A" OR L$>"Z" THEN 250
270 PRINT L$:PRINT
297 REM
298 REM---------------------CHECK GUESS
299 REM
300 M=0:FOR N=1 TO LEN(GL$)
310 IF L$=MID$(GL$,N,1) THEN M=1
```

```
320 NEXT N:IF M=0 THEN 400
330 PRINT"YOU TRIED THAT ALREADY. "
340 GOTO 470
400 GL$=GL$+L$:M=0:FOR N=1 TO LW
410 IF MID$(SW$,N,1)=L$ THEN GOSUB 900
420 NEXT N:IF M>0 THEN 490
430 WG=WG+1:GOSUB 2000:PRINT"WRONG! ";
440 PRINT 10-WG;"GUESS";
450 IF WG<9 THEN PRINT"ES";
460 PRINT" LEFT.    "
470 LOCATE 1,1
480 GOTO 200
490 PRINT"RIGHT!                  "
495 RG=RG+M:GOTO 470
497 REM
498 REM---------------------PLAYER WINS
499 REM
500 PRINT:PRINT:PRINT
510 PRINT"CONGRATULATIONS! YOU WIN."
520 GOTO 650
597 REM
598 REM--------------------PLAYER LOSES
599 REM
600 PRINT:PRINT:PRINT
610 PRINT"SORRY -- YOU LOSE.     ":PRINT
620 PRINT"THE WORD WAS ";SW$;"."
650 PRINT:PRINT"PLAY AGAIN?"
660 A$=INKEY$
670 IF A$="Y" THEN RUN
680 IF A$="N" THEN END
690 GOTO 660
897 REM
898 REM-----------INSERT GUESSED LETTER
899 REM
900 M=M+1:LF$="":RI$=""
910 IF N>1 THEN LF$=LEFT$(DW$,N-1)
920 IF LW>N THEN RI$=RIGHT$(DW$,LW-N)
930 DW$=LF$+L$+RI$:RETURN
997 REM
998 REM--------------------SECRET WORDS
999 REM
1000 DATA ONYX,JILT,TRYST,QUICK,BLITZ
```

```
1010 DATA AGUE,EERIE,QUILT,QUARTZ,OXEN
1020 DATA RHYTHM,ONLY,DWELL,STRIFE
1030 DATA STRAIGHT,AXLE,GROMMET,THROUGH
1040 DATA ROUGHLY,IDIOCY,DIZZIER,JUGGLE
1050 DATA IMMENSELY,FROTH,WHEEDLED
1060 DATA KNOCKING,WHARVES,LAUGHTER
1990 DATA X
1997 REM
1998 REM--------------------DRAW GALLOWS
1999 REM
2000 ON WG GOTO 2050,2100,2200,2300
2010 ON WG-4 GOTO 2400,2500,2600
2020 ON WG-7 GOTO 2700,2800,2900
2050 A=X+(10*K4)-(3*K3)
2060 FOR B=A TO A+(10*K3) STEP K3
2070 POKE B,K5:NEXT B:RETURN
2100 FOR B=X TO X+(K4*9) STEP K4
2110 POKE B,K5:NEXT B:RETURN
2200 FOR B=X TO X+(K3*6) STEP K3
2210 POKE B,K5:NEXT B:RETURN
2300 A=X+K4+(6*K3)
2310 FOR B=A TO A+(2*K4) STEP K4
2320 POKE B,73-K7:NEXT B:RETURN
2400 POKE B,79-K7:RETURN
2500 B=B+K4
2510 POKE B,K5:POKE B+K4,K5:RETURN
2600 POKE B-K3,61:RETURN
2700 POKE B+K3,61:RETURN
2800 B=B+(2*K4)
2810 POKE B-K3,60:RETURN
2900 POKE B+K3,62:RETURN
8997 REM
8998 REM-------------CONVERSION ROUTINE
8999 REM
9000 K0=
9010 K1=
9020 K2=
9030 K3=
9040 K4=
9050 K5=
9060 K6=
```

```
9070 K7=

     (If your
     conversion
     routine requires
     extra lines,
     add them here.
     See Chapter 12.)

9200 RETURN
```

# CHAPTER 17
# HUNT THE SNAKE

This is one of those violent video games that moral crusaders complain about. You see a snakelike shape slithering realistically around your video screen, twisting and turning in a random pattern. Your aim is to move a marker to hit the snake on the head. As soon as you succeed, you continue to the next level of difficulty, in which you hunt the snake all over again . . . except that it is now a *shorter* snake, as if you chopped off a piece of it the first time around. As you continue from one level to the next, the snake gets shorter and shorter, until it is reduced to a pitiful paraplegic blob.

Does this game encourage cruelty to snakes? After playing it, will you want to go and knock something (or someone) on the head? Alternatively, will an hour or two spent gazing into the video screen and tapping the computer keyboard act as an *outlet* for all those aggressive impulses, leaving you in a relaxed, pacific state, feeling nothing but love for all living things? Be sure to write to your local anti-video-game crusaders and let them know.

## How to Use It

After displaying the game instructions, the program asks you to type one of your initials. This will be used as your marker on the screen while the game is running. You will control its position by typing 1, 2, A, or Z to move left, right, up, or down, respectively.

The snake appears on the screen, grows to its full length, and starts slithering around. You must try to move your marker to hit the very first segment of the snake; otherwise, the game won't register a hit.

At level one, the snake is 15 segments long. It doesn't change direction too often, and you have ample time to hit it. At higher levels, the snake is shorter, it changes direction frequently, and the time counts down much faster.

If the time counts down to zero before you get the snake, you lose—but only at that level. You can play it again right away. Your score, which accumulates from one level to the next, is directly related to how quickly you get the snake. The maximum possible score, if you win at all the levels of the game, is about 6ØØ points. A score of 4ØØ is good.

You can alter this game to start with a longer or shorter snake—or impose a different time limit; see "Going Further," p. 163.

When typing this program, note that letter **I** is used to represent the code of the player's initial. Don't type a numeral **1** by mistake.

## Adapting It for Your Computer

You *must* add a conversion routine on lines 9ØØØ through 92ØØ for this program to work. Check Chapter 12 for the conversion routine appropriate to your computer.

The word **CLS** appears on lines 2Ø, 51Ø, 64Ø, and 11ØØ. The expression **A$=INKEY$** occurs on lines 15Ø, 31Ø, and 9ØØ. If your computer doesn't understand either of these statements, check Chapter 2 for a substitute. If you have an Apple II, line 31Ø must look like this:

```
31Ø PP=PEEK(K9):POKE K8,Ø:A$="":IF PP>K6
    THEN A$=CHR$(PP+K7)
```

The statement **LOCATE 1,1** appears on lines 21Ø and 116Ø to home the cursor without clearing the screen. Check Chapter 2 to see if your computer uses a different statement for this. If your computer does not allow you any substitute at all, you won't be able to display the time and score while the game is running, and you should omit lines 21Ø, 22Ø, 116Ø, 117Ø, and 118Ø.

IBM users should type a different line 22Ø:

**22Ø LOCATE 1,5: PRINT STR$(T);" ";**

Users of the TRS-8Ø should type **RND(Ø)** instead of **RND(1)** in the expression on line 4ØØ.

When you run the program, if it does not generate a border of asterisks around the edge of the video screen, you need to alter line 2Ø3Ø. Instead of **E=42** type **E=42-K7** on that line.

Users of the Apple II will need to alter the POKE and PEEK statements on lines 24Ø, 25Ø, 26Ø, 36Ø, 37Ø, 39Ø, 41Ø, 61Ø, 62Ø, and 121Ø. For the Apple II, type the following lines:

```
24Ø POKE VM%(S(N)),K6
25Ø IF PEEK(VM%(S(N-1)+DS))=E THEN GOSUB 4ØØ
26Ø S(N)=S(N-1)+DS:POKE VM%(S(N)),K5
36Ø IF PEEK(VM%(X+DX))=E THEN DX=Ø
37Ø IF DX<>Ø THEN POKE VM%(X),K6:X=X+DX
39Ø POKE VM%(X),I
41Ø IF PEEK(VM%(S(N-1)+DS))=E THEN DS=-DS
61Ø POKE VM%(S(A)),K6:FOR N=1 TO 1ØØ:NEXT N
62Ø POKE VM%(S(A)),I:FOR N=1 TO 1ØØ:NEXT N
121Ø POKE VM%(C),E
```

Be careful to type them correctly. One error can stop the program. Be sure to save your program before you run it.

## How It Works

Generally speaking, any BASIC game that uses POKE statements to move more than a couple of graphics symbols around the screen will be too slow to be interesting. Yet the snake in this game starts out 15 units long and seems to move quite quickly. How is it done?

The secret is that the "body" of the snake isn't moving at all. All that happens, in each cycle of the program, is that one segment at the end of the snake is blanked out, and a new segment is added at the front.

Important variables include:

**SC:** Score
**LV:** Level of game
**LS:** Initial length of snake
**TL:** Time limit
**S( ):** Location of each snake segment, from one to **LS**
**X:** Player's position
**DX:** Player's direction of movement
**DS:** Snake's direction of movement
**CY:** Cumulative number of cycles of snake movement
**NC:** Number of cycles at which new **DS** is needed
**I:** Player's initial
**E:** ASCII code of screen border
**W:** Win/lose indicator

Line by line, the program works like this:

30–140

After **GOSUB 9000** activates the conversion routine, **GOSUB 2000** sets some constants that will be used in all levels of the game. Then instructions are displayed, and the player is asked to type an initial.

150–190

The keyboard is scanned until one character, from A to Z, is typed. Meanwhile, the RND function is read repeatedly to advance it to a fresh value. The ASCII code of the player's initial is assigned to **I.** **GOSUB 1000** resets the game for the next level; see lines 1000–1040.

200

A loop begins, counting down from the time limit to zero. All game action is contained within this loop, so the game sequence recycles with a NEXT statement instead of a GOTO statement that would take longer to execute.

210–220

At the start of each main cycle, the time **T** is decremented and displayed.

230–240

The snake moves a distance equal to its own length (one "snake loop") in each cycle of the main "time loop" of the program. The snake loop takes longer when the snake is longer, so the time loop counts down more slowly in lower levels of the game. The tail-end snake segment is erased with **K6,** a blank space.

250

Before adding a new segment at the snake's front end, the program checks whether this video location is on the edge of the playing area. If so, subroutine 400 is used to find a new value for **DS.**

260

Tail segment **N** is moved to a position **DS** units from the head segment **N-1.**

270

If the number of cycles has exceeded the limit, **GOSUB 400** chooses a new random direction for the snake.

300–370

The keyboard is scanned for player instructions. Player direction **DX** is adjusted accordingly. If the player tries to move the marker into the screen border, **DX** is reset to 0. If **DX<>0**, the player's marker is blanked and its location is updated.

380

If the new location of the player's marker coincides with the head segment of the snake, the game is won. Both loops (the snake loop and time loop) must be terminated; it is not good practice to jump out of an incomplete loop with a GOTO, so the two loop variables **N** and **T** are set to their final values, after having had their current values assigned to **A** and **B**, respectively, for future reference.

390–395

The player's initial is POKEd into video memory. The loops are incremented. If they have both reached their final values, either because of a win or because time has run out, execution jumps to line 500.

400–420

A new direction is chosen for the snake. If this will lead it into the edge of the playing area, the new direction is reversed. Because the snake doesn't spontaneously change direction until **NC** cycles after the last change, **NC** being set to slightly more than half the length of the snake, it can never run into its own body, and this possibility does not need to be checked.

1000–1040

The game level is increased by 1, the length of the snake decreased by 1, and **NC** reset to match. Initial video positions are calculated to suit any display. Each segment of the snake is assigned a video address. Other variables are reset.

1100–1180

A border is drawn around the edge of the screen,

beginning from video address **C.** Along each edge, **A** is the number of segments of the border, **B** the increment. The loop in subroutine 2000 creates the image.

## Going Further

The game has been designed so that you can easily change the initial length of the snake and the time allowed to score a hit. On line 2010, **LS=16** defines the length of the snake; type a number larger or smaller than 16 if you wish. Very long snakes will not move interestingly on the screen, since the snake always hits an edge before it has time to choose a new random direction.

On line 2020, **TL** is the time limit—the figure from which the time begins counting down at each level. Type a higher number than 50 if you want more time, or a lower number if you want less.

On line 2030, **E** is the ASCII code that creates the border around the edge of the screen. If you don't like asterisks, type a number other than 42 on this line. Don't use the same code as the value of **K5,** which forms the body of the snake.

If you know how to save data onto disk or tape, you could consider adapting this program so that it saves the score of each person who has used it. This would make it more like a real arcade game, with a chart listing high scores to date.

```
10 REM                      HUNT THE SNAKE
20 CLS
30 GOSUB 9000:GOSUB 2000
35 PRINT"IN THIS GAME, A SNAKE CRAWLS"
40 PRINT"AROUND THE SCREEN WHILE YOU"
45 PRINT"CHASE AFTER IT.":PRINT
50 PRINT"YOU MUST KNOCK IT ON THE"
55 PRINT"HEAD TO WIN THE GAME.":PRINT
60 PRINT"THE FASTER YOU PLAY, THE MORE"
65 PRINT"YOU SCORE. EACH TIME YOU WIN,"
70 PRINT"YOU CAN GO ON TO A NEW LEVEL"
75 PRINT"WITH A SHORTER, FASTER SNAKE."
80 PRINT:PRINT"THERE ARE 15 LEVELS."
85 PRINT
90 PRINT"TO MOVE YOUR MARKER:":PRINT
100 PRINT"  1=LEFT"
110 PRINT"  2=RIGHT"
120 PRINT"  A=UP"
130 PRINT"  Z=DOWN":PRINT
140 PRINT"TYPE YOUR INITIAL TO BEGIN:";
150 A$=INKEY$
160 R=RND(1)
170 IF A$<"A" OR A$>"Z" THEN 150
180 PRINT A$:I=ASC(A$)-K7
190 GOSUB 1000
197 REM
198 REM----------SHOW SCORE, MOVE SNAKE
199 REM
200 FOR T=TL TO 0 STEP -1
210 LOCATE 1,1
220 PRINT TAB(4);STR$(T);" "
230 S(0)=S(LS):FOR N=1 TO LS
240 POKE S(N),K6
250 IF PEEK(S(N-1)+DS)=E THEN GOSUB 400
260 S(N)=S(N-1)+DS:POKE S(N),K5
270 CY=CY+1:IF CY>NC THEN GOSUB 400
297 REM
298 REM---------------------MOVE PLAYER
299 REM
300 DX=0
310 A$=INKEY$
320 IF A$="1" THEN DX=-K3
```

```
330 IF A$="2" THEN DX=K3
340 IF A$="A" THEN DX=-K4
350 IF A$="Z" THEN DX=K4
360 IF PEEK(X+DX)=E THEN DX=Ø
370 IF DX<>Ø THEN POKE X,K6:X=X+DX
380 IF X=S(N) THEN W=1:A=N:N=LS:B=T:T=Ø
390 POKE X,I
395 NEXT N:NEXT T:GOTO 5ØØ
397 REM
398 REM-------------NEW SNAKE DIRECTION
399 REM
4ØØ DS=SGN(RND(1)-.5)*(DC-ABS(DS))
41Ø IF PEEK(S(N-1)+DS)=E THEN DS=-DS
42Ø CY=Ø:RETURN
497 REM
498 REM------------------PLAYER LOSES
499 REM
5ØØ IF W=1 THEN 6ØØ
51Ø CLS
52Ø PRINT"YOU RAN OUT OF TIME"
53Ø PRINT"AT LEVEL";LV;".":PRINT
54Ø PRINT"YOUR SCORE IS STILL";SC;"."
55Ø PRINT:PRINT"TRY AGAIN?"
56Ø GOSUB 9ØØ:IF A$="N" THEN END
57Ø GOSUB 1Ø1Ø:GOTO 2ØØ
597 REM
598 REM-------------------PLAYER WINS
599 REM
6ØØ FOR M=1 TO 5
61Ø POKE S(A),K6:FOR N=1 TO 1ØØ:NEXT N
62Ø POKE S(A),I:FOR N=1 TO 1ØØ:NEXT N
63Ø NEXT M
64Ø CLS
65Ø PRINT"YOU WIN AT LEVEL";LV;"!"
66Ø SC=SC+B:IF LS=1 THEN 7ØØ
67Ø PRINT:PRINT"YOUR NEW SCORE:";SC
68Ø PRINT:PRINT"TRY THE NEXT LEVEL?"
69Ø GOSUB 9ØØ:IF A$="N" THEN END
695 GOSUB 1ØØØ:GOTO 2ØØ
697 REM
698 REM-------------------END OF GAME
699 REM
```

```
700 PRINT:PRINT"THAT WAS THE LAST"
710 PRINT"LEVEL. YOU KILLED THE SNAKE."
720 PRINT:PRINT"YOUR FINAL SCORE:";SC
730 END
897 REM
898 REM----------------------YES/NO INPUT
899 REM
900 A$=INKEY$
910 IF A$<>"Y" AND A$<>"N" THEN 900
920 RETURN
997 REM
998 REM------------RESET FOR NEXT LEVEL
999 REM
1000 LV=LV+1:LS=LS-1:NC=INT(LS/2)+2
1010 X=K0+K4*INT(.3*K2)+K3*INT(.3*K1)
1020 B=K0+K4*INT(.7*K2)+K3*INT(.5*K1)
1030 FOR A=1 TO LS:S(A)=B+(K3*A):NEXT A
1040 CY=0:W=0:DX=0:DS=K3
1097 REM
1098 REM-------------------SCREEN LAYOUT
1099 REM
1100 CLS
1110 C=K0+K4
1120 A=K1-1:B=K3:GOSUB 1200
1130 A=K2-2:B=K4:GOSUB 1200
1140 A=K1-1:B=-K3:GOSUB 1200
1150 A=K2-2:B=-K4:GOSUB 1200
1160 LOCATE 1,1
1170 PRINT"TIME";TAB(12);"SCORE";SC;
1180 PRINT TAB(24)"LEVEL";LV
1190 RETURN
1195 REM-----
1200 FOR N=1 TO A
1210 POKE C,E
1220 C=C+B:NEXT N:RETURN
1997 REM
1998 REM-------------------SET CONSTANTS
1999 REM
2000 DC=K4+K3:SC=0:LV=0
2010 LS=16:DIM S(LS)
2020 TL=50
2030 E=42
```

```
2040 RETURN
8997 REM
8998 REM--------------CONVERSION ROUTINE
8999 REM
9000 K0=
9010 K1=
9020 K2=
9030 K3=
9040 K4=
9050 K5=
9060 K6=
9070 K7=

     (If your
     conversion
     routine
     requires
     extra lines,
     add them here.
     See Chapter 12.)

9200 RETURN
```

# PART 6
# SIMULATION

# CHAPTER 18
# RAT RACE

This program is much longer and more complicated than the others. It is more versatile and interesting to use, however, and it develops some of the real potential in BASIC.

It's a tongue-in-cheek simulation of the life of a stereotypical, hard-pressed male corporate executive, trying to maximize his income, career success, domestic bliss, and other pleasures, while minimizing high blood pressure, ulcers, exhaustion, obesity, and overwork. The player has to choose from a series of daily options, such as passing the buck, tax evasion, business lunches, or flirting with a female secretary. Each option affects different score categories; for instance, a business lunch increases the "career success" score but also increases "ulcer" and "obesity" ratings. Too much indulgence of this kind can lead to serious health problems! Likewise, having an affair with a secretary can lead to divorce, and tax evasion can result in fines or jail.

## How to Use It

After displaying instructions, the program sets up the screen with a series of lines showing the initial amounts of wealth, success, ulcers, obesity, and so on, in bar-chart format.

The bar at the top of the chart shows the total score.

When this bar grows all the way across the screen, you win. Take as long as you like, and make as many choices as you like, but be warned—the longer the game lasts, the more chance there is of you encountering bleeding ulcers, a heart attack, bankruptcy, or a nervous breakdown, any one of which is liable to be fatal.

Before typing this program, either you should have had some experience using BASIC elsewhere, or you should have typed and used some of the simpler programs in this book.

## Adapting It for Your Computer

No conversion routine is needed at the end of this program because no graphics are involved.

The word **CLS** is used on lines 17Ø and 5ØØØ. The expression **A$=INKEY$** appears on line 8ØØ. If your computer doesn't understand these terms, check Chapter 2 for possible substitutes.

The statement **LOCATE 1,1** is used on lines 4Ø5 and 91Ø. Check Chapter 2 to see if your computer uses a substitute statement. Some computers allow you no substitute at all, in which case you must omit lines 4Ø5 and 91Ø completely. The program won't look as good without them, but it will run adequately.

Users of IBM computers should insert a semicolon after the symbols **SP$** on line 9ØØ of the program.

TRS-8Ø users should type **RND(Ø)** instead of **RND(1)** in the expression on line 52Ø.

If you are a slow typist, you can reduce the length of this program by leaving out some of the DATA statements beginning on line 6ØØØ. These statements are divided into sections, each prefaced by a heading such as BREAKFAST OPTIONS or MORNING OPTIONS. There are 2Ø options in each section, and 6 separate sections. You may omit up to 1Ø options from each section. You must omit *the same number* of options from each section. You must also omit the set of letters on each DATA line immediately below each omitted option. Then, instead of the number 2Ø on line 52ØØ, type the new number of options that you are using in each section of DATA. You must also type this number instead of 2Ø in the RND statement on line 52Ø.

The only disadvantage of having fewer DATA statements is that the program won't display as many different daily options and won't seem so varied or realistic.

## How It Works

Since the DATA and setup routines take a lot of room, I've put them at the end of the program, beginning on line 5ØØØ.

After the **GOSUB 5ØØØ** statement has been executed, lines 4Ø through 15Ø display instructions. Then the "daily decision cycle" starts on lines 2ØØ through 26Ø. These lines control the rest of the program.

Line 2ØØ tells the computer to **GOSUB 4ØØ.** The routine beginning on line 4ØØ displays the current scores on the screen in bar-chart form. The program checks to see if the value of the first bar in the chart equals 24. This first bar is the total score, and 24 is its maximum value. If **V(1)=24,** the player has won.

Otherwise, the program checks all the other score values, **V(2)** through **V(16).** The first 1Ø of these are displayed on the screen, while the rest are hidden from the player. This is the complete list:

A. **V(1)** = Aggregate score
B. **V(2)** = Wealth
C. **V(3)** = Success
D. **V(4)** = Domestic bliss
E. **V(5)** = Other pleasure
F. **V(6)** = Work load

G. **V(7)** = Ulcers
H. **V(8)** = Obesity
I. **V(9)** = Exhaustion
J. **V(1Ø)** = Blood pressure
K. **V(11)** = Compliance toward employers
L. **V(12)** = Kindness to subordinates
M. **V(13)** = Attention to wife's needs
N. **V(14)** = Attention to kids' needs
O. **V(15)** = Infidelity
P. **V(16)** = Dishonesty

The names of the first 1Ø categories appear as DATA statements on lines 55ØØ through 559Ø. Quote marks are required in these statements to preserve the leading and trailing spaces that make the video layout look right.

If wealth, success, domestic bliss, or other pleasures fall too low, the program issues warnings. The initial minimum levels for these scores are 6 units, listed in the DATA statement on line 57ØØ.

When work load, ulcers, obesity, exhaustion, or blood pressure rises too high, other warnings are issued. The maximum levels for these factors are initially set at 11, 12, 11, 11, and 11 units; see the DATA on lines 57ØØ and 571Ø.

The hidden factors, stored in variables **V(11)** through **V(16)**, result in nasty surprises—just as in real life. The player's attitude toward employers, employees, wife, and kids can be either positive or negative; that is, values **V(11)** through **V(14)** can be positive or negative. If the score gets too far out of line either way, a warning occurs.

The infidelity and dishonesty values **V(15)** and **V(16)** are updated each time the player chooses to flirt with a secretary or indulge in unscrupulous business practices.

Lines 22Ø through 25Ø in the daily decision cycle compare the current score values with warning levels specified by **WL(1)** through **WL(16).** Any value that's over its limit results in a GOSUB **1000**, to display warnings specified in lines 1250 through 2244. The warning level is then reset to a slightly higher value. After 3 warnings in any major category, the player loses the game.

Having checked all the score values, the program adds 1 to the value of **T**, which is the time-of-day counter. There are 6 times of day (see DATA statements on lines 5600 through 5650). After late evening, a new day begins all over again with breakfast.

Line 260 of the daily decision cycle activates subroutine **500**, which picks 4 options randomly from the 20 available in each time of day. These options are displayed on the screen.

Depending on which option the player chooses, different score values go up and down, determined by code letters that are linked with that option. For example, on line 6140, the option ALLOW SON A DAY OFF SCHOOL is followed by code letters **DN-M.** Each letter before the hyphen tells the computer to *increase* the corresponding score category. Letter **B** identifies category **V(2), C** identifies category **V(3),** and so on. **DN-M** therefore tells the computer to increase score category **V(4),** which is domestic bliss, and category **V(14),** attention to kids' needs.

The hyphen acts as a minus sign, telling the computer to *decrease* categories listed subsequently. In this case, **−M** decreases the score in category **V(13),** attention to wife's needs, the logic being that the executive's wife may resent his giving her the chore of looking after the son on his day off from school.

Some options increase score categories by more than 1 point. STEAL SECRETS FROM COMPETITOR, for instance, is such a major decision that it increases wealth by 2 points (the secrets will net the executive some sort of dividend), career success by 5 points, and ulcers by 1 point (because dishonesty involves risk, risk involves worry, and worry creates ulcers). The dishonesty rating increases by 2 points. Work load diminishes by 4 points (because theft of ideas is a substitute for hard work), and exhaustion diminishes by 1 point (less honest toil).

When playing the game, you can try for a quick win via such dishonest options—hoping that wealth and success stay ahead of sharply rising health risks and legal penalties. Or you can opt for slower, duller options, such as PASS THE BUCK, which slightly increases career success while diminishing work load, ulcers, exhaustion, and blood pressure. It also diminishes the amount of consideration shown toward subordinates, but the penalties for this are less severe than the penalties for fraud.

## Going Further

If you disagree with the rewards and penalties that follow each option, you can adjust them to suit yourself. For instance, GET UP EARLY AND JOG increases exhaustion by 2 points, while reducing obesity and blood pressure by 1 point each. Check the complete range of categories listed in "How It Works" and decide which ones should be affected.

There must be at least one code letter on the DATA line following each option in the list beginning on line 6ØØØ.

Bear in mind that if you remove too many negative consequences, the game will become too easy. As it stands, a cautious player should be able to win about 1 time in 4.

You can substitute different daily options instead of the ones I have listed. I'm not a corporate executive myself; if you are, you may know of some daily options that I've unwittingly left out. Substitute yours for any of my options that don't appeal to you;

change the code letters accordingly to add and subtract points in appropriate categories.

Finally, you can enlarge some of the messages that appear on the screen. I have tried to keep them short to save you as much typing as possible. Some, such as YOU CONTRACT PERITONITIS. IT'S FATAL are little more than telegrams. The simulation will be more vivid if you add extra words to these messages. This will be easy if your video display allows you more than 4Ø characters per line.

I had fun writing "Rat Race," and my friends have had fun playing it. If you enjoy it, too, you should consider writing a simulation of your own using the same techniques. Imagine a situation and the factors that determine how that situation changes. Imagine all the possible actions and all the possible results. Use variables to keep track of each quantity. You may also need a formula to link your variables. Write down all the options, and decide how much to reveal to the player while the simulation is running. You'll need to play it many times, adjusting the different factors, to make the game realistic. If your computer allows easy graphics, consider adding them, too.

For just a few hundred dollars, a modern home computer offers the same computing power that once cost *hundreds of thousands* of dollars. If you use it merely to play prepackaged video games, you aren't taking advantage of all that power. A simulation game is one good way of exploring the real potential of microcomputing.

```
1Ø REM                                  RAT RACE
2Ø REM
3Ø GOSUB 5ØØØ
4Ø PRINT"YOU ARE A HARASSED EXECUTIVE"
```

```
50 PRINT"TRYING TO ACCUMULATE MONEY,"
60 PRINT"STATUS, MARRIED BLISS, AND"
70 PRINT"OTHER PLEASURES, AVOIDING"
80 PRINT"ULCERS, OBESITY, EXHAUSTION,"
90 PRINT"& HIGH BLOOD PRESSURE.":PRINT
100 PRINT"CHOOSE DAILY OPTIONS WITH"
110 PRINT"CARE, TO MAXIMIZE YOUR SCORE"
120 PRINT"AND MINIMIZE YOUR CHANCES OF"
130 PRINT"BANKRUPTCY, UNEMPLOYMENT,"
140 PRINT"DIVORCE, OR DEATH!":PRINT
150 PRINT"PRESS ANY KEY TO BEGIN."
160 GOSUB 800
170 CLS
197 REM
198 REM------------DAILY DECISION CYCLE
199 REM
200 GOSUB 400:IF V(1)=24 THEN 300
210 FOR W=2 TO 5
220 IF V(W)<WL(W) THEN GOSUB 1000
230 NEXT W:FOR W=6 TO 16
240 IF ABS(V(W))>WL(W) THEN GOSUB 1000
250 NEXT W:T=T+1:IF T=7 THEN T=1
260 GOSUB 500:GOTO 200
297 REM
298 REM---------------------PLAYER WINS
299 REM
300 GOSUB 910:GOSUB 900
310 PRINT L$:PRINT"CONGRATULATIONS!"
320 PRINT L$:PRINT
330 PRINT"YOU'VE WON THE RAT RACE."
340 GOTO 3020
397 REM
398 REM---------------------SCORE CHART
399 REM
400 RESTORE
405 LOCATE 1,1
410 FOR N=1 TO 10:IF N=6 THEN PRINT
420 READ A$:PRINT A$;
430 IF V(N)=0 THEN 450
440 PRINT LEFT$(PA$,V(N));
450 IF V(N)=24 THEN 470
460 PRINT LEFT$(CO$,24-V(N));
```

```
470 PRINT:NEXT N:PRINT:PRINT:PRINT
480 RETURN
497 REM
498 REM-----------------MENU OF OPTIONS
499 REM
500 GOSUB 900:PRINT TAB(7);T$(T);":"
510 PRINT:PRINT TAB(7);L$:FOR N=1 TO 4
520 R=INT(RND(1)*20)+1:IF N=1 THEN 560
530 A=0:FOR M=1 TO N-1
540 IF R=CH(M) THEN A=1
550 NEXT M:IF A=1 THEN 520
560 PRINT"    ";N;" ";OP$(T,R):CH(N)=R
570 NEXT N:PRINT TAB(7);L$
597 REM
598 REM-----------------PLAYER'S CHOICE
599 REM
600 PRINT:PRINT TAB(7)"YOUR CHOICE:";
610 GOSUB 800
620 IF A$<"1" OR A$>"4" THEN 610
630 PRINT A$;:B=CH(VAL(A$))
640 C=1:FOR N=1 TO LEN(RE$(T,B))
650 A=ASC(MID$(RE$(T,B),N,1))
670 IF A=45 THEN C=-1:GOTO 720
680 A=A-64:V(A)=V(A)+C
690 IF V(A)<0 THEN V(A)=0
700 IF V(A)>24 THEN V(A)=24
720 NEXT N
730 V(1)=INT((V(2)+V(3)+V(4)+V(5))/3)-2
740 IF V(1)>24 THEN V(1)=24
750 RETURN
797 REM
798 REM-------------------KEYBOARD SCAN
799 REM
800 A$=INKEY$
810 IF A$="" THEN R=RND(1):GOTO 800
820 RETURN
897 REM
898 REM----------------SCREEN CLEARANCE
899 REM
900 FOR N=1 TO 10:PRINT SP$:NEXT
910 LOCATE 1,1
920 FOR N=1 TO 14:PRINT:NEXT:RETURN
```

```
997 REM
998 REM------------------------WARNINGS
999 REM
1000 GOSUB 910:GOSUB 900
1010 PRINT"WARNING !!!":PRINT:PRINT L$
1020 NW(W)=NW(W)+1:A=W-1:GOSUB 1200
1040 PRINT L$:PRINT:WL(W)=B
1050 IF A$="" THEN 1080
1060 RE$(T,0)=A$:B=0:GOSUB 640
1080 PRINT"PRESS ANY KEY TO CONTINUE."
1090 GOSUB 800:GOSUB 400:RETURN
1199 REM
1200 ON A GOTO 1250,1300,1350,1400,1450
1210 A=A-5
1220 ON A GOTO 1500,1550,1600,1650,1700
1230 A=A-5
1240 ON A GOTO 1800,1900,2000,2100,2200
1250 REM-------------------------WEALTH
1260 ON NW(W) GOTO 1270,1280,1290
1270 PRINT"NOT ENOUGH CASH. YOU ASK"
1272 PRINT"YOUR WIFE TO FIND A JOB."
1274 B=6:A$="BBBBBGIJ-DDMM":RETURN
1280 PRINT"YOU'RE DANGEROUSLY SHORT OF"
1282 PRINT"MONEY. TRY HARDER, OR ELSE!"
1284 B=4:A$="BBGGIIJ-EF":RETURN
1290 PRINT"SO DEEP IN DEBT, YOU END UP"
1292 PRINT"BANKRUPT.":GOTO 3000
1300 REM------------------------SUCCESS
1310 ON NW(W) GOTO 1320,1330,1340
1320 PRINT"YOU'RE NOT VERY SUCCESSFUL."
1322 PRINT"YOU HAVE TO TRY HARDER."
1324 B=6:A$="CCGIJ-E":RETURN
1330 PRINT"YOUR BOSS IS WONDERING IF"
1332 PRINT"YOU CAN HANDLE THIS JOB."
1334 PRINT"TRY HARDER -- OR ELSE!"
1336 B=4:A$="BCGGIIJ-E":RETURN
1340 PRINT"YOU'RE A FAILURE AT WORK,"
1342 PRINT"THEY FIRE YOU.":GOTO 3000
1350 REM-----------------MARRIED BLISS
1355 V(13)=0:V(14)=0
1360 ON NW(W) GOTO 1370,1380,1390
1370 PRINT"NOT ENOUGH DOMESTIC BLISS:"
```

```
1372 PRINT"SPEND MORE TIME AT HOME."
1374 B=6:A$="DDDDFFMN-CCEIIJ":RETURN
1380 PRINT"AVOID DOMESTIC STRIFE AND"
1382 PRINT"DIVORCE! PAMPER YOUR WIFE."
1384 B=4:A$="DDDDIJMM-CCC":RETURN
1390 PRINT"YOU NEGLECTED YOUR DOMESTIC"
1392 PRINT"LIFE. YOUR WIFE HAS WALKED"
1394 PRINT"OUT ON YOU.":GOTO 3000
1400 REM------------------OTHER PLEASURES
1410 ON NW(W) GOTO 1420,1430,1440
1420 PRINT"YOU'RE DEPRIVING YOURSELF"
1422 PRINT"OF PLEASURES OUTSIDE HOME"
1424 PRINT"AND WORK. ENJOY LIFE MORE!"
1426 B=5:A$="EEEF-CCGG":RETURN
1430 PRINT"YOU HAVE SO FEW PLEASURES,"
1432 PRINT"YOU'RE VERY DEPRESSED. BE"
1434 PRINT"CAREFUL YOU DON'T CRACK UP."
1436 B=4:A$="E-C":RETURN
1440 PRINT"SO FEW PLEASURES, YOU SHOOT"
1442 PRINT"YOURSELF.":GOTO 3000
1450 REM-----------------------WORK LOAD
1460 ON NW(W) GOTO 1470,1480,1490
1470 PRINT"WORK LOAD IS OUT OF HAND."
1472 PRINT"CANCEL YOUR VACATION."
1474 A$="BBBCCCGIIIJ-DDDEMN"
1476 V(6)=7:B=12:RETURN
1480 PRINT"REDUCE YOUR WORK LOAD!"
1482 PRINT"WORK LATE EVERY NIGHT."
1484 A$="BBBCCCGIIIJ-DDEEMN"
1486 V(6)=11:B=16:RETURN
1490 PRINT"WORK LOAD OUT OF CONTROL!"
1492 PRINT"YOU'RE FIRED. YOU START A"
1494 PRINT"NEW JOB FOR LESS PAY."
1496 A$="GGG-BBBBBCCCCCDE"
1498 V(6)=0:B=10:WL(W)=0:RETURN
1500 REM--------------------------ULCERS
1510 ON NW(W) GOTO 1520,1530,1540
1520 PRINT"ULCER TROUBLE! DRUGS HELP,"
1522 PRINT"BUT YOU MUST DO LESS WORK."
1524 B=14:V(7)=8
1526 A$="DEFFFF-CCIIJ":RETURN
1530 PRINT"HOSPITALIZED WITH ULCERS!"
```

```
1532 PRINT"YOU WERE WARNED TO TAKE IT"
1534 PRINT"EASY. TAKE TWO WEEKS OFF."
1536 A$="FFFFF-BBCCEIJ":V(7)=11
1538 B=2Ø:RETURN
154Ø PRINT"ULCERS START BLEEDING."
1542 PRINT"YOU CONTRACT PERITONITIS."
1544 PRINT"IT'S FATAL.":GOTO 3ØØØ
155Ø REM------------------------OBESITY
156Ø ON NW(W) GOTO 157Ø,158Ø,159Ø
157Ø PRINT"YOU'VE PUT ON WEIGHT. YOU"
1572 PRINT"MUST DIET, BUT IT DEPRESSES"
1574 PRINT"YOU, SO YOU DRINK MORE."
1576 A$="FGGGJ-CDDE":V(8)=7:B=14:RETURN
158Ø PRINT"OVERWEIGHT AGAIN!"
1582 PRINT"GO TO A HEALTH SPA."
1584 A$="FFFF-BBCEEIIIJJ":V(8)=12
1586 B=15:RETURN
159Ø PRINT"SO FAT, YOUR WIFE THREATENS"
1592 PRINT"TO LEAVE, SECRETARY BREAKS"
1594 PRINT"OFF HER AFFAIR. DIET AGAIN."
1596 A$="JJ-DDDEEE":V(8)=8:V(15)=Ø
1598 B=13:NW(8)=INT(RND(1)*2):RETURN
16ØØ REM---------------------EXHAUSTION
161Ø ON NW(W) GOTO 162Ø,163Ø,164Ø
162Ø PRINT"YOU'RE EXHAUSTED. IGNORE"
1622 PRINT"JOB AND FAMILY FOR A WEEK."
1624 A$="EEFFFFH-CCCDDDGGJJMN"
1626 V(9)=7:B=16:RETURN
163Ø PRINT"HOSPITALIZED WITH NERVOUS"
1632 PRINT"EXHAUSTION. TAKE IT EASY!"
1634 A$="FFFFHH-BBCCCJ"
1636 V(9)=14:B=2Ø:RETURN
164Ø PRINT"EXHAUSTION! YOU CRACK UP."
1642 PRINT"YOU'RE FIRED.":GOTO 3ØØØ
165Ø REM-----------------BLOOD PRESSURE
166Ø ON NW(W) GOTO 167Ø,168Ø,169Ø
167Ø PRINT"YOUR BLOOD PRESSURE'S HIGH."
1672 PRINT"YOU MUST TAKE TIME OFF."
1674 A$="FFFGH-CC":B=14:V(1Ø)=9:RETURN
168Ø PRINT"BLOOD PRESSURE CAUSES HEART"
1682 PRINT"ATTACK! REST AND AVOID"
1684 PRINT"STRESS IN FUTURE--OR ELSE!"
```

```
1686 A$="FFFG-CCCII":B=20:V(10)=12
1688 RETURN
1690 PRINT"YOU DIDN'T LISTEN, DID YOU?"
1692 PRINT"BLOOD PRESSURE CAUSES FATAL"
1694 PRINT"HEART ATTACK.":GOTO 3000
1700 REM--------------------OBEY BOSS
1710 B=2:IF V(11)<0 THEN 1750
1720 PRINT"YOU'RE GIVEN MORE PAY AND"
1725 PRINT"EXTRA WORK BECAUSE YOU'VE"
1730 PRINT"TRIED SO HARD AT YOUR JOB."
1735 A$="BBBCCFFFFGGIIJ":V(11)=0:RETURN
1750 PRINT"YOUR INDEPENDENT, ABRASIVE"
1755 PRINT"ATTITUDE AT WORK GETS YOU"
1760 PRINT"DEMOTED, PLUS EXTRA TASKS."
1765 A$="FFFFGGII-CCC":V(11)=0:RETURN
1800 REM--------------EASY ON EMPLOYEES
1810 B=2:IF V(12)<0 THEN 1850
1815 PRINT"YOU'RE SO NICE TO EMPLOYEES"
1820 PRINT"THEY TAKE ADVANTAGE. YOU'RE"
1825 PRINT"BLAMED WHEN OUTPUT SLUMPS."
1830 A$="FFFFGGII-CCC":V(12)=0:RETURN
1850 PRINT"EMPLOYEES HATE YOUR TOUGH"
1855 PRINT"POLICIES, BUT OUTPUT RISES."
1860 PRINT"YOU REAP THE CREDIT."
1870 A$="BBBBCCCE-FFGIJ":V(12)=0:RETURN
1900 REM------------------NICE TO WIFE
1905 B=3:IF V(13)<0 THEN 1950
1910 PRINT"YOU'VE BEEN SO NICE TO YOUR"
1915 PRINT"WIFE, SHE TAKES ADVANTAGE"
1920 PRINT"AND GOES ON SPENDING SPREE."
1930 A$="GJ-BDE":V(13)=0:RETURN
1950 PRINT"YOUR WIFE'S NEEDS HAVE NOT"
1955 PRINT"BEEN MET. SHE ABANDONS"
1960 PRINT"YOU FOR A WEEK."
1970 A$="GGIIJ-DDDEE":V(13)=0:RETURN
2000 REM--------------PERMISSIVE PARENT
2010 B=2:IF V(14)<0 THEN 2050
2015 PRINT"YOU'VE BEEN SO NICE TO YOUR"
2020 PRINT"KIDS THEY'VE BECOME SPOILED"
2025 PRINT"BRATS. BE MORE STRICT."
2030 A$="GIJ-DD":V(14)=0:RETURN
2050 PRINT"YOU'VE BEEN TOO TOUGH WITH"
```

```
2055 PRINT"YOUR KIDS. THEY REBEL, USE"
2060 PRINT"DRUGS, AND ARE ARRESTED."
2065 A$="GGIJ-BDDDE":V(14)=0:RETURN
2100 REM-----------------------INFIDELITY
2104 V(15)=0
2105 ON NW(W) GOTO 2110,2120,2130
2110 PRINT"YOUR WIFE SUSPECTS YOU OF"
2112 PRINT"INFIDELITY. WATCH OUT!"
2114 A$="GGJ-DDDDEE":B=2:RETURN
2120 PRINT"YOUR WIFE FINDS OUT ABOUT"
2122 PRINT"YOUR SECRET AFFAIR. STOP"
2124 PRINT"NOW, BEFORE IT'S TOO LATE!"
2126 A$="GGJ-DDDDDEEE":B=2:RETURN
2130 PRINT"YOU PLAYED AROUND ONCE TOO"
2132 PRINT"OFTEN! YOUR WIFE SUES FOR"
2134 PRINT"DIVORCE!":GOTO 3000
2200 REM-----------------------DISHONESTY
2205 V(16)=0
2210 ON NW(W) GOTO 2220,2230,2240
2220 PRINT"YOUR BOSS SUSPECTS YOU OF"
2222 PRINT"UNETHICAL BUSINESS CONDUCT."
2224 PRINT"NO PROMOTION FOR YOU!"
2226 A$="GJ-BBCCCCCE":B=2:RETURN
2230 PRINT"YOUR ILLEGAL PRACTICES ARE"
2232 PRINT"UNCOVERED. YOU ALMOST LOSE"
2234 PRINT"YOUR JOB. BE MORE CAREFUL!"
2236 A$="GGJ-BBBCCCCCE":RETURN
2240 PRINT"ARRESTED FOR TAX FRAUD AND"
2242 PRINT"INDUSTRIAL ESPIONAGE, YOU"
2244 PRINT"ARE THROWN IN JAIL."
2997 REM
2998 REM---------------------PLAYER LOSES
2999 REM
3000 PRINT L$:PRINT
3010 PRINT"TOO BAD--YOU LOSE!"
3020 PRINT"DO YOU WANT TO TRY AGAIN?"
3030 GOSUB 800:IF A$="N" THEN END
3040 RUN
4997 REM
4998 REM-------------INITIAL SUBROUTINE
4999 REM
5000 CLS
```

```
5Ø1Ø PRINT"READING DATA":PRINT
5Ø2Ø FOR N=1 TO 13:SP$=SP$+"   ":NEXT
5Ø3Ø L$="--------------------------"
5Ø4Ø PA$="))))))))))))))))))))))))))"
5Ø5Ø CO$=":::::::::::::::::::::::::"
5Ø6Ø DIM V(16),WL(16),NW(16),CH(4)
5Ø7Ø DIM OP$(6,2Ø),RE$(6,2Ø),T$(6)
51ØØ FOR N=1 TO 1Ø:READ A$:NEXT N
511Ø FOR N=1 TO 6:READ T$(N):NEXT N
512Ø FOR N=1 TO 16:READ WL(N):NEXT N
513Ø FOR N=1 TO 1Ø:V(N)=8:NEXT N
52ØØ FOR M=1 TO 6:FOR N=1 TO 2Ø
521Ø READ OP$(M,N):READ RE$(M,N)
522Ø NEXT N:NEXT M
53ØØ RETURN
5499 REM
55ØØ DATA "   TOTAL SCORE "
551Ø DATA "         WEALTH "
552Ø DATA "        SUCCESS "
553Ø DATA "DOMESTIC BLISS "
554Ø DATA "OTHER PLEASURE "
555Ø DATA "      WORK LOAD "
556Ø DATA "         ULCERS "
557Ø DATA "        OBESITY "
558Ø DATA "     EXHAUSTION "
559Ø DATA "BLOOD PRESSURE "
5599 REM
56ØØ DATA AT BREAKFAST
561Ø DATA IN THE MORNING
562Ø DATA AT YOUR MID-DAY BREAK
563Ø DATA DURING THE AFTERNOON
564Ø DATA IN THE EARLY EVENING
565Ø DATA DURING LATE EVENING
5699 REM
57ØØ DATA Ø,6,6,6,6,11,12,11
571Ø DATA 11,11,1,1,3,1,3,2
5997 REM
5998 REM--------------BREAKFAST OPTIONS
5999 REM
6ØØØ DATA GET UP EARLY AND JOG
6ØØ5 DATA II-HJ
6Ø1Ø DATA DRINK SEVERAL CUPS OF COFFEE
```

```
6Ø15 DATA GGJ-I
6Ø2Ø DATA HURRY OFF EARLY TO THE OFFICE
6Ø25 DATA BCCGIJ-DEFF
6Ø3Ø DATA SLEEP IN FOR AN EXTRA HOUR
6Ø35 DATA EEH-CIIJ
6Ø4Ø DATA TELL WIFE SHE MUST ECONOMIZE
6Ø45 DATA BB-DD
6Ø5Ø DATA AGREE TO A VACATION IN EUROPE
6Ø55 DATA DDEEFFMN-BBBGIJ
6Ø6Ø DATA AGREE TO GO AWAY THIS WEEKEND
6Ø65 DATA DEFM-BGIJ
6Ø7Ø DATA IMPOSE HOME SPENDING CUTS
6Ø75 DATA BBJJ-DM
6Ø8Ø DATA EAT A LARGE NUTRITIOUS MEAL
6Ø85 DATA EHH-GGI
6Ø9Ø DATA COOK BREAKFAST FOR THE FAMILY
6Ø95 DATA DDIIJMN-E
61ØØ DATA AGREE TO MOVE TO LARGER HOME
61Ø5 DATA CCDDEG-BBB
611Ø DATA MAKE EARLY BUSINESS CALLS
6115 DATA BCCI-DEFF
612Ø DATA GIVE KIDS EXTRA $$ ALLOWANCE
6125 DATA DDN-B
613Ø DATA AGREE TO BUY A NEW CAR
6135 DATA DDE-BB
614Ø DATA ALLOW SON A DAY OFF SCHOOL
6145 DATA DN-M
615Ø DATA SIT AND READ WALL ST. JOURNAL
6155 DATA BCCE-D
616Ø DATA GIVE WIFE BREAKFAST IN BED
6165 DATA DDDIIMM-E
617Ø DATA AGREE TO HAVE HOUSE REPAINTED
6175 DATA DDGM-BB
618Ø DATA MAKE KIDS HELP WITH CHORES
6185 DATA DM-IN
619Ø DATA SEND SQUABBLING KIDS UPSTAIRS
6195 DATA -IJN
6197 REM
6198 REM-----------------MORNING OPTIONS
6199 REM
62ØØ DATA FLATTER CORPORATION PRESIDENT
62Ø5 DATA BCCJK-F
```

```
6210 DATA BRAVELY CONFRONT YOUR BOSS
6215 DATA IJJ-K
6220 DATA TELL BOSS HOW SHREWD HE IS
6225 DATA BCCK-F
6230 DATA CATCH UP ON CORRESPONDENCE
6235 DATA CI-FF
6240 DATA VISIT PSYCHOTHERAPIST
6245 DATA DF-BGIJ
6250 DATA FIRE A LAZY ASSISTANT
6255 DATA CJ-FLL
6260 DATA SNEAK OUT FOR A QUIET STROLL
6265 DATA EEFF-CGHIJ
6270 DATA SPEND AN HOUR SCHEMING
6275 DATA BCEF-I
6280 DATA CALL STOCKBROKER FOR ADVICE
6285 DATA BBBC
6290 DATA CALL STOCKBROKER FOR ADVICE
6295 DATA G-BB
6300 DATA WARN LAZY WORKERS TO SHAPE UP
6305 DATA CJ-IL
6310 DATA FLIRT WITH SECRETARY
6315 DATA EEO
6320 DATA KISS SECRETARY IN XEROX ROOM
6325 DATA EEOOJ
6330 DATA GIVE SECRETARY SOME ROSES
6335 DATA EO-F
6340 DATA UNLOAD CHORES ONTO SECRETARY
6345 DATA CC-FFIL
6350 DATA PLAN AN AMBITIOUS NEW PROJECT
6355 DATA BBCCFFGIIJK
6360 DATA STEAL SECRETS FROM COMPETITOR
6365 DATA BBCCCCCPP-FFFFI
6370 DATA SUBMIT PADDED EXPENSE ACCOUNT
6375 DATA BBBBP
6380 DATA STEAL CREDIT FOR ASST'S WORK
6385 DATA BCCCP-FFIL
6390 DATA ASK ACCOUNTANT RE TAX EVASION
6395 DATA BBBBCGPP
6397 REM
6398 REM-----------------MIDDAY OPTIONS
6399 REM
6400 DATA BUSINESS LUNCH WITH COLLEAGUE
```

```
6405 DATA BCCEGHHJ
6410 DATA ROMANTIC LUNCH WITH SECRETARY
6415 DATA OEEH-B
6420 DATA BRIBE RETAILER W. FANCY LUNCH
6425 DATA BCCHHG-F
6430 DATA GET HAPPILY DRUNK
6435 DATA EEEEGHHJ-II
6440 DATA WORK THRU LUNCH AT THE OFFICE
6445 DATA BCCCGIJ-EFFF
6450 DATA CUDDLE W. SECRETARY IN OFFICE
6455 DATA EEJO
6460 DATA TAKE AN EXTRA HOUR OVER LUNCH
6465 DATA EFHH-CGIK
6470 DATA EAT COTTAGE CHEESE AND SALAD
6475 DATA I-EHHJJ
6480 DATA MAKE FOND PHONE CALL TO WIFE
6485 DATA DDM
6490 DATA SKIP LUNCH; VISIT HEALTH CLUB
6495 DATA CI-GHHJ
6500 DATA MAKE EVERYONE WORK THRU LUNCH
6505 DATA BCCIJ-FFKLL
6510 DATA GIVE EMPLOYEES AFTERNOON OFF
6515 DATA FFLL-C
6520 DATA SNOOP AROUND EMPTY OFFICES
6525 DATA BCCP
6530 DATA NAP ON YOUR OFFICE COUCH
6535 DATA EH-CIJ
6540 DATA SIT IN THE PARK OGLING GIRLS
6545 DATA EEJ-I
6550 DATA DREAM UP BOGUS TAX DEDUCTIONS
6555 DATA BBBBGP
6560 DATA BUY WIFE AN EXPENSIVE GIFT
6565 DATA DDM-B
6570 DATA BUY KIDS A NEW TOY
6575 DATA DDN-B
6580 DATA BLACKMAIL A BUSINESS ENEMY
6585 DATA BBBBCCCCGJPP-FFF
6590 DATA BUY JEWELRY FOR SECRETARY
6595 DATA EO-B
6597 REM
6598 REM---------------AFTERNOON OPTIONS
6599 REM
```

```
66ØØ DATA THREATEN TO QUIT
66Ø5 DATA BCCGJJ-KK
661Ø DATA ACCEPT A NEW RESPONSIBILITY
6615 DATA BCCFFGK
662Ø DATA PASS THE BUCK
6625 DATA C-FFGGIJL
663Ø DATA AGREE TO TAKE ON EXTRA WORK
6635 DATA BCCFFGIIK
664Ø DATA PINCH SECRETARY'S BOTTOM
6645 DATA EEO
665Ø DATA ISSUE MERIT-PAY BONUSES
6655 DATA BCLL-F
666Ø DATA INSTITUTE SALARY CUTBACKS
6665 DATA CCJ-LL
667Ø DATA DELEGATE TOIL TO SUBORDINATES
6675 DATA CE-FFFGIIL
668Ø DATA SMEAR THE RECORD OF A RIVAL
6685 DATA BBCCCEP-F
669Ø DATA EMBEZZLE CORPORATE FUNDS
6695 DATA BBBBBBBBCCEEGPPP-FF
67ØØ DATA DO ISOMETRIC EXERCISES
67Ø5 DATA I-H
671Ø DATA SET UP A DATE WITH SECRETARY
6715 DATA EEO
672Ø DATA JOB INTERVIEW AT RIVAL CORP.
6725 DATA CC
673Ø DATA DEMAND A LARGE PAY INCREASE
6735 DATA BBBCJ-KK
674Ø DATA GET SOMEONE TO SPY ON A RIVAL
6745 DATA BBCCCCCP-FF
675Ø DATA SET UP KICKBACK WITH SUPPLIER
6755 DATA CCBBBBP
676Ø DATA MASTERMIND A NEW PRODUCT LINE
6765 DATA BCCCFFGIJ-K
677Ø DATA REORGANIZE A WHOLE DEPARTMENT
6775 DATA BCCGIJ-FFKL
678Ø DATA CALL A MEETING
6785 DATA CFH-GIJ
679Ø DATA COMPUTERIZE YOUR DEPARTMENT
6795 DATA BCFFFFGGGGIIIJJ
6797 REM
6798 REM-----------------EVENING OPTIONS
```

```
6799 REM
6800 DATA PLY SECRETARY WITH BOOZE
6805 DATA EEEGHJO-BII
6810 DATA WORK AT THE OFFICE TILL 7:30
6815 DATA BCCIIK-DE
6820 DATA HURRY HOME TO BE WITH FAMILY
6825 DATA DDEM-CGIJ
6830 DATA TAKE WORK HOME WITH YOU
6835 DATA BCCI-DEFF
6840 DATA MAKE EVERYONE WORK OVERTIME
6845 DATA CIJ-FFL
6850 DATA VISIT MARRIAGE COUNSELLOR
6855 DATA DDDH-BGO
6860 DATA LET SUBORDINATES LEAVE EARLY
6865 DATA FLL-CK
6870 DATA SEE BOSS FOR DRINK AFTER WORK
6875 DATA BCCGHH-DI
6880 DATA END AFFAIR WITH SECRETARY
6885 DATA BBGJJ-EEEEEOOOOOOOOOO
6890 DATA TAKE SECRETARY TO A MOTEL
6895 DATA EEEEEEEEDIJOOO-H
6900 DATA UNWIND ALONE AT A LOCAL BAR
6905 DATA GH-DII
6910 DATA SECRETLY MEET INDUSTRIAL SPY
6915 DATA BBBCCCCCGP-FF
6920 DATA FALL ASLEEP ON TRAIN HOME
6925 DATA EE-GII
6930 DATA DRINK WITH PALS ON TRAIN HOME
6935 DATA EEGHHJ-I
6940 DATA WORK ON THE TRAIN HOME
6945 DATA BCCIJ-FF
6950 DATA FLIRT WITH WOMAN ON THE TRAIN
6955 DATA EE-I
6960 DATA TREAT FAMILY TO A FANCY MEAL
6965 DATA DDEHHMN-BGI
6970 DATA LISTEN TO YOUR WIFE GOSSIP
6975 DATA DGGIIJJM
6980 DATA COOK DINNER FOR YOUR FAMILY
6985 DATA DDIIM-E
6990 DATA REFUSE TO TALK TO WIFE & KIDS
6995 DATA -DDGIIJJMN
6997 REM
```

```
6998 REM--------------------NIGHT OPTIONS
6999 REM
7ØØØ DATA DO KIDS' HOMEWORK FOR THEM
7ØØ5 DATA DIN-E
7Ø1Ø DATA VISIT MOTHER-IN-LAW WITH WIFE
7Ø15 DATA DIIJMM-EEE
7Ø2Ø DATA HANG OUT AT A LOCAL TAVERN
7Ø25 DATA EEGH-DII
7Ø3Ø DATA WORK ALONE IN YOUR STUDY
7Ø35 DATA BCCI-DFF
7Ø4Ø DATA ALLOW SON TO BORROW YOUR CAR
7Ø45 DATA DGGN
7Ø5Ø DATA ATTEND PTA MEETING
7Ø55 DATA DIJ-E
7Ø6Ø DATA SECRET TRYST WITH SECRETARY
7Ø65 DATA EEEEEEEEDIJOOO-H
7Ø7Ø DATA SEND KIDS TO BED EARLY
7Ø75 DATA EJ-NI
7Ø8Ø DATA WATCH BASEBALL AND DRINK BEER
7Ø85 DATA EGHH-IIJ
7Ø9Ø DATA FLIRT WITH DIVORCEE NEXT DOOR
7Ø95 DATA EEEO-D
71ØØ DATA GIVE A GARAGE SALE
71Ø5 DATA BBDI-E
711Ø DATA TAKE WIFE & KIDS OUT BOWLING
7115 DATA DEIMN-BH
712Ø DATA WORK LATE WHILE WIFE SLEEPS
7125 DATA BCCII-DDEM
713Ø DATA GET DRUNK AND PASS OUT
7135 DATA EEGG-DIIIM
714Ø DATA YOU AND WIFE TO BED EARLY
7145 DATA DDDEEM-GHHIJ
715Ø DATA SECRETLY TELEPHONE SECRETARY
7155 DATA EEEGO
716Ø DATA LIE AWAKE MAKING JOB PLANS
7165 DATA BCCII
717Ø DATA GET UP AND WORK AT 3 AM
7175 DATA BCCIIG-FF
718Ø DATA WIFE'S TUPPERWARE PARTY
7185 DATA DDMIJJ-EEE
719Ø DATA PLAY SOFTBALL WITH KIDS
7195 DATA DDEEIN-HHHJ
```